Family-tested tips and techniques for getting the services your child needs

FOR PARENTS, GRANDPARENTS GUARDIANS AND PROFESSIONALS

Team Up For Your Child

A Step-By-Step Guide to Working Smarter with Doctors, Schools, Insurers, and Agencies

By Wendy Lowe Besmann

In consultation with:

William Allen, PhD	Monica Causey, CMSW	Melissa Massie, MS
William Berez, PhD	Sita Diehl, MA, MSSW	Carletta Rando-Smelcer, MA
Brian Bonfardin, MD	Joshua Gettinger, MD	Ronda Redden Reitz, PhD
Drema Bowers, MSSW	Jim Griffin, MSSW, LCSW	Karen Sowers, PhD
Donna Flanery	Lynne F. Harmon, MA, CCC-SLP	Mike Sterling, MSSW, LCSW
Bobby Brown, MSSW, LCSW	Barbara Levin, MD, MPH	Nicole Swain, PsyD
Charlotte Bryson, MA	Debby Lovin-Buuck, MSSW, LCSW	Anne Burnett Young, MS, CAS
Archie Carden, EdD	Karen Loy, EdD	

Sponsored By:

Melton Hill Media
Oak Ridge, Tennessee
www.meltonhillmedia.com

Copyright © 2008, Wendy Lowe Besmann

All rights reserved

The information in this volume is intended to be advice from families for the benefit of families. It is not a substitute for consultation with a qualified healthcare or educational provider.

No part of this book may be reproduced, translated, stored in a retrieval system, or transmitted in any form or by any means without written permission from Melton Hill Media, LLC. For reprint and other permissions, contact permissions@meltonhillmedia.com.

Printed in the United States of America.

This book is printed on acid-free paper.

Last digit is print number: 9 8 7 6 5 4 3 2 1

Published by Melton Hill Media, LLC
9119 Solway Ferry Road
Oak Ridge, TN 37830
www.meltonhillmedia.com

Library of Congress Cataloging-in-Publication Data

Besmann, Wendy Lowe

Team Up for Your Child: A Step-By-Step Guide to Working Smarter with Doctors, Schools, Insurers, and Agencies

Includes bibliographical references

ISBN-10: 0-9816793-0-7 ISBN-13: 978-0-9816793-0-3

1. Parenting–Psychology–Education
2. Special needs–popular works

Library of Congress Control Number: 2008904916

"At last, the 'owner's manual' families need! Countless NAMI families have asked for a road map to getting services for their children. **Team Up for Your Child** helps parents and other caregivers steer a course to finding help and support. Easy to use, this workbook takes you step by step through the process of getting mental health, educational, and other services for your child. It helps you walk into meetings calm and prepared. Many thanks to Wendy Besmann for translating the wisdom she has gained in her personal experience into a guidebook for all of us."

—Sita Diehl, Executive Director, NAMI (National Alliance on Mental Illness) Tennessee

Team Up for Your Child was originally developed as a Tennessee-based pilot project to help families work more effectively with medical, behavioral health, and educational professionals. The project was sponsored by NAMI Tennessee with support from 16 health, education, and community donors. We gratefully acknowledge the role of these organizations in helping to make this book possible:

- Cherokee Health Systems
- Child and Family Tennessee
- East Tennessee Children's Hospital
- Family Practice Associates
- Helen Ross McNabb Center
- Katharine Collins Roddy and J.P. Roddy, Sr. Fund of East Tennessee Foundation
- Knox County Schools
- Janssen Pharmaceutica
- Magellan Health Services Tennessee Care Management Center
- Mental Illness Awareness Coalition
- NAMI Knoxville
- Parent-Child Services Group, Inc.
- Peninsula
- Project GRAD Knoxville
- Ridgeview Resources for Living
- Tennessee Voices for Children

The manuscript for this book was reviewed numerous times by the 23 health and education professionals listed on the cover. Their expertise has been invaluable. Heartfelt thanks, too, for the efforts of Mary Linda Schwarzbart, who provided grants consultancy and computer technical support. You can read more about them on the next page.

Finally, I wish to thank my family—Ted, Anna, David and Greta Besmann—for their loving encouragement, and for the many fascinating life lessons they have taught me over the years.

I hope this book makes your life easier! I'd love to hear from you at: wendy@meltonhillmedia.com.

Wendy Lowe Besmann

About the Author

Wendy Lowe Besmann is a writer, an advocate for mental health services, and the mother of a teenager with autism and bipolar disorder. A freelance journalist and editor for more than 30 years, she has contributed articles to national publications that include *Better Homes and Gardens, USA Today, The New York Times, SELF, Travel & Leisure, Atlantic Monthly, Esquire,* and *Parenting*. She is also the author of **A Separate Circle** (University of Tennessee Press, Knoxville, Tennessee, 2000). Besmann is president of NAMI Knoxville. She serves on the Tennessee Department of Mental Health and Developmental Disability's State Mental Health Planning and Policy Council, the Knox Youth Transition Council, and the advisory council of the Knox County Family Support Network.

Advisory Committee

William Allen, PhD, is Vice President for Children's Services of Cherokee Health Systems.

William Berez, PhD, is the Chief Clinical Officer for Cherokee Health Systems.

Brian Bonfardin, MD, is a psychiatrist on the Clinical Faculty of East Tennessee State University's Department of Psychiatry.

Drema Bowers, MSSW, is the Director of Campus Family Support for Project GRAD Knoxville.

Donna Flanery is the former On-TRAC Facilitator for Support and Training for Exceptional Parents, Inc. (STEP, Inc.).

Bobby Brown, MSSW, LCSW, is the Clinical Director of Peninsula Hospital in Louisville, Tennessee.

Charlotte Bryson, MA, is Executive Director of Tennessee Voices for Children.

Archie Carden, EdD, is a psychologist for the Tennessee Department of Children's Services.

Monica Causey, CMSW, is Project Director of Tennessee Parent Information and Resources Center with Tennessee Voices for Children.

Sita Diehl, MA, MSSW, is Executive Director of NAMI Tennessee.

Joshua Gettinger, MD, is a family physician and co-owner of Family Practice Associates in Monroe County, Tennessee.

Jim Griffin, MSSW, LCSW, is a Family Outreach Specialist with Tennessee Voices for Children.

Lynne F. Harmon, MA, CCC-SLP, is President of Parent-Child Services Group, Inc.

Barbara Levin, MD, MPH, is Medical Director of the Monroe County Health Council and the Women's Wellness Maternity Center, and is the Public Health Officer for Loudon County, Tennessee.

Debby Lovin-Buuck, MSSW, LCSW, is Field Network Coordinator for Magellan Health Services Tennessee Care Management Center.

Karen Loy, EdD, is the principal of Ridgedale Alternative School, which provides comprehensive diagnostic and behavioral programs for Knox County Schools in Knoxville, Tennessee.

Melissa Massie, MS, is Director of Pupil Personnel for Knox County Schools.

Carletta Rando-Smelcer, MA, is Program Coordinator for Helen Ross McNabb Center.

Ronda Redden Reitz, PhD, is a clinical psychologist in private practice.

Karen Sowers, PhD, is Dean of the University of Tennessee's College of Social Work.

Mike Sterling, MSSW, LCSW, is Director of the Intensive Focus Group Program at Ridgeview Psychiatric Hospital.

Nicole Swain, PsyD, is a clinical and pediatric psychologist for East Tennessee Children's Hospital.

Anne Burnett Young, MS, CAS, is a Certified Addiction Specialist in Knoxville, Tennessee.

Acknowledgements

Illustration, design, and production by Barbara Boeing, Boeing Design & Illustration, bboeing@frontiernet.net. Copy-editing by Em Turner Chitty, Em Turner English Services, etenglish@yahoo.com. Grants consultation and computer technical support by Mary Linda Schwarzbart, CSD of Knoxville, Inc., marylinda@comcast.net. Special thanks to Roger Stewart of NAMI Tennessee, John McCook of Knox County Schools, Janice Cook of Knox County Schools, Jerry Hodges of Project GRAD Knoxville, and Linda Zweifel of NAMI Montgomery County, Texas for technical assistance and encouragement.

Copyright © 2008, Wendy Lowe Besmann. All rights reserved except as expressly assigned by the author. No part of this workbook or CD may be copied for other than personal use without written permission from the author. For more information, contact meltonhillmedia@yahoo.com.

For Parents, Grandparents, Guardians, and Professionals

Team Up For Your Child

A Step-By-Step Guide to Working with Medical, Behavioral Health, and Educational Professionals

Table of Contents

Chapter 1: The Big Picture .... page 4
How to use this book…symbols to guide you…your child's strengths and needs…the first diagnosis…what to know about medical, behavioral health, and developmental specialists.

Chapter 2: Getting Prepared .... page 11
Listing your child's symptoms…record-keeping made easier… health history forms…making sense of reports and evaluations… understanding the treatment plan.

Chapter 3: Working with the Team .... page 35
Tips for good communication…making the most of appointment time…keeping your whole team informed…what to do if someone's not listening…practicing assertiveness.

Chapter 4: Tracking Your Child's Progress .... page 47
How to be a good observer…avoiding medication mixups… easy ways to record results…side-effects checklist…giving and getting information between visits.

Chapter 5: The Classroom-Treatment Connection .... page 54
How special education works…translating the IEP…how to be a full partner in a school meeting…the most effective goals… transitioning with your teen…what teachers wish you knew.

Chapter 6: Insurance Companies and Social Agencies .... page 80
Doorways to health care benefits…how managed care works… what's "medically necessary?"…tips for dealing with customer service.

Chapter 7: Coping with Crisis and Healing the Family .... page 88
When things fall apart…Family crisis survival kit…Twenty questions to ask when your child needs hospitalization…how to lower the stress on siblings…widening your circle of support.

Chapter 8: Glossary .... page 94
Common terms used by medical, behavioral health, and educational professionals.

Chapter 9: Where to Learn More .... page 99
Sources of information, support, skills, and strategies for taking care of your family and yourself.

Chapter 1
The Big Picture

For All Kinds of Parents

*The term **parent** in this book is meant to include the increasing number of grandparents, other relatives, legal guardians, and foster parents who face the challenge of raising children with behavioral health issues.*

How to Use This Book

When a child has serious behavioral issues, the parent's world is turned upside down. In this new world, most of the ordinary rules for raising kids don't seem to work. Something's wrong, but you don't know why or what to do. You're stressed out, angry, confused, and scared.

At first, you might hope the problem will just go away. You think: *Maybe there's not enough discipline in this house. Maybe it's a phase. Maybe it's because we moved...got divorced...had a big change in our lives. Maybe it's the teacher. Or those kids down the block. Maybe everything will be okay if...* (fill in the blank).

Still, the tension is always there. Who knows what will set off the next crisis? You worry about what will happen in the future. You worry about all the simple, fun things your child is missing. As time goes on, you start to feel cut off from that other world of "normal" families whose kids seem to act in ways that other people understand.

Meanwhile, you suddenly have a team of "professionals" in your life who provide services for your child. Their language is filled with long, unfamiliar words. People with clipboards ask a lot of personal questions. You read forms, fill out forms, and sign more forms. And one thing you can count on in this strange new world: People who don't have to go home with your child will keep telling you to be patient! (Unfortunately, they are often right.)

Building a New Kind of Normal

At age three our son was diagnosed with autism and bipolar disorder. For the next dozen years, life in our house was tough. Day after day, we coped with a child who would suddenly explode in a fit of scratching, kicking, and biting. He couldn't hold a real conversation, couldn't have friends. He spent a week in a psychiatric hospital. We jumped every time the phone rang on a school day, because it usually meant bad news. And like most such families, we grieved for the "normal" life we couldn't have.

Little by little, something changed. We learned to reach out for help. With good treatment, our son's behavior improved. We learned ways to enjoy ourselves, and to make the hard parts a lot easier. Like so many families who share this struggle, we learned that our job was to build a *new kind of normal* that makes sense for the life we live.

Most of all, we learned how to join that team of medical, behavioral, and educational professionals as full, working partners. It can be tempting to let the experts do it all. The reality is, they can't do it alone. Most children don't improve very much unless their families take an active role. In fact, the best way to get through this strange new world is by learning how to work with your

Those L-o-o-n-g, Confusing Words

Medical, behavioral health, and educational professionals can use a lot of technical language. For plain definitions of words printed like this *in the pages of* **Team Up for Your Child,** *see Chapter 8, "Glossary."*

•

Different organizations may use different terms. Sometimes behavioral health is called "mental health" and a behavioral health issue may be called a "mental illness." A behavioral health issue that seriously disrupts a child's life may be called a "Serious Emotional Disturbance (SED)." ADHD or developmental disorders such as autism can also create behavioral health problems that need treatment.

---

team. All you really need to start are the right tools and the will to hang in there. That's what this book is all about–finding simple ways to get involved.

Who's on Your Team?

"Behavioral health" is a way to describe a person's emotions, actions, and ability to manage everyday activities. A behavioral health problem can affect your child at home, in school, or in many other parts of life. That's why your child's team may have a lot of members. These may include several doctors and therapists, health workers, or a case manager. Other members of the team may work for government agencies, the school system, or an insurance program. You might deal with some of these people only a few times and deal with others for many years.

No matter what titles these professionals wear, the real coach of this team is YOU, the parent. Our health and educational system can be so disconnected that the other members need YOU to make sure they work together. Each professional helps with different parts of your child's situation. Quite often they aren't able to talk with each other very easily. YOU are the only one who takes care of the whole child. That doesn't mean you have to run everything or know everything. You can't be an expert on every part of your child's treatment or education. Your job is to keep track of the Big Picture—and make sure everybody else sees it, too.

***Team Up for Your Child* is a step-by-step guide to working with your child's team of professionals.** It's full of ideas from other parents, worksheets to help you get organized, and sources for learning more. It's meant to be used over and over again. The symbols listed on the next page will help you find the tools you need.

You can flip through the pages to pick out sections that are most useful right now. You can use the worksheets in this book as a convenient place to keep the records and notes you'll need when you talk to professionals on the team.

(If you prefer to keep information on your computer, the worksheets in this book are available on a CD in form-fill PDF format. Go to www.meltonhillmedia.com for details.)

Living with a child who has a behavioral health issue is never easy. Every day, we're all just trying to figure things out. *Team Up for Your Child* can help you break down what may seem like a big awful mess into small tasks you can handle. You CAN do it—and only you can do it!

–Wendy Lowe Besmann

1 The Big Picture
CONTINUED

Download, Fill In, Save Data

An e-book version of **Team Up For Your Child**, as well as a CD with all the worksheets in this book, can be purchased at www.meltonhillmedia.com.

Symbols in This Book

 Keywords and definitions of common terms you may encounter in dealing with professionals, schools, insurance companies, and others

 Good ideas tested by other parents

 Helpful Internet sites

 Useful material in print

 Important alerts

 More on the next page

 Lists or sample forms to fill in

 File this paperwork in your 3-ring binder

 Tips

 Información disponible en español

My Child's Strengths and Needs

The lists on the next two pages can help you consider some general areas you need to discuss with health and education professionals. Think about your child's physical and emotional health. Consider daily behavior, school performance, and relationships with friends, family, or teachers. Don't forget likes and dislikes, activities, and interests.

Also, consider asking friends, relatives, teachers or others in the community to make suggestions. Sometimes other people in your child's life can help you see the Big Picture more clearly. **Go to Chapter 7 for more ideas on finding your "Circle of Support."**

My child's strengths:
_____
_____
_____

Things about my child that concern me:
Right now:
_____
_____
_____
_____
_____
_____
_____

In the next two or three years:
_____
_____
_____
_____
_____
_____

When my child is an adult:
_____
_____
_____
_____

How This Can Help

The list on this page can help you start thinking about the "symptoms" you'll describe in Chapter 2. Some of what you write here may be private, but other parts can be shared with professionals who help your child. The whole team needs to know how YOU see this child's present and future.

1 The Big Picture
CONTINUED

How I Picture the Best My Child Can Be:

My child's daily behavior at home would look like:
_____
_____
_____
_____
_____
_____
_____

Success at school for my child would be:
_____
_____
_____
_____

My child's social life and friendships would look like:
_____
_____
_____
_____
_____

My child's free-time activities would look like:
_____
_____
_____
_____

Our life as a family would look like:
_____
_____
_____
_____
_____

Hope Makes Things Happen

The right treatment can make big changes in your child's life. Try picturing that life as if it were scenes from a movie you'd like to watch. What would these scenes look like?

You aren't just daydreaming. Looking at the Big Picture means trying to define what your child can do and be. Some of these hopes will help the team set long-term goals.

In this box, paste a happy picture of your child. The whole team is working for this!

Other hopes, plans, and dreams for our child and our family's future:

_____
_____
_____
_____
_____
_____

Other things I want people who work with us to know about my child and our family:

_____
_____
_____
_____
_____
_____
_____
_____
_____
_____

Listen to Your Child, Too

Consider asking your child to list strengths, concerns, and hopes for the future. You can use the questions on the next page or change them to fit the child's age and ability to pay attention.

This also offers a good chance to talk to your child about receiving treatment. Explain that giving this information will help the people who provide treatment to understand the situation a little better. If possible, promise that you won't judge or respond negatively to anything the child chooses to say.

Copy the next page, so the child isn't influenced by what you've written above. (Many older children may prefer to fill out the lines on the next page by computer. You can get a CD with the worksheets by going to www.meltonhillmedia.com.)

For a young child, you can read the questions and fill in answers, doing a little at a time. You might let the child add more information through drawing pictures. Even if only one or two questions are completed, it's important to let your child have a voice in this process.

1 The Big Picture
CONTINUED

"My Space"

On this sheet, write down some things you want people to know about you. Everybody has things they like about themselves and their lives. Everybody has things they wish they could change. People in your life may already be asking you some of these questions. It's good to think about them on your own time, so you can say what you really mean. Your feelings and needs matter! Knowing what you want will make it easier to get the help you need.

My name is: _____

Some things I like to do are:
_____
_____
_____

Things I like best about myself:
_____
_____
_____

Things I worry about sometimes:
_____
_____
_____

Things I do sometimes, but I don't know why:
_____
_____
_____

I feel most unhappy when I:
_____
_____
_____

If I could change something about my life or myself, it would be:
_____
_____
_____

What really makes me feel good is:
_____
_____
_____

In the future, I hope I can:
_____
_____
_____

Chapter 2
Getting Prepared

The Big Book

To make a diagnosis, most behavioral health professionals use the **Diagnostic and Statistical Manual of Mental Disorders** *(DSM), by the American Psychiatric Association. This book lists the symptoms usually seen in each type of disorder. A child must meet a certain number of symptoms listed in order to receive that diagnosis. Most local libraries will have a copy of the DSM. You may be able to purchase a used version at www.amazon.com.*

The First Diagnosis

Most parents begin with a pressing need to know "What's wrong with our child? What do we CALL it?" We feel as if putting a label on this strange behavior will give us some power to find the magic cure. The trouble is that a child's behavior is never a perfect match with any label. A `diagnosis` is the overall term that health professionals use to describe a problem. The diagnosis is reached through an `evaluation` of your child's behavior and emotions. `Evidence` may come from conversations with you, your child, and others. Other facts may come from a physical examination, tests, or laboratory studies. The evaluation and diagnosis will be used to plan treatment and inform others on the team. They may also be used to decide if your child can get certain mental health expenses paid by your insurance. In some cases, they will help decide whether your child can receive special services at school.

A diagnosis is a guideline, not a recipe. Each child's brain, experiences, and emotions are different. Those differences will affect the kinds of medications or therapy that work best. Sometimes, a child meets some of the `criteria` (types of behavior) for another disorder, which will be called a **secondary** or `comorbid` diagnosis. The diagnosis may change as your child grows or as more information is gathered.

Where to Start

The first step is to have the child examined by a `primary care doctor.` This person is sometimes known as a "family doctor," "primary care practitioner," or "family medicine practitioner." This doctor may also be called a PCP, or "primary care provider" for insurance purposes. The primary care doctor may be a `pediatrician,` a medical doctor specializing in children's overall health care. In some cases, you will see a `Nurse Practitioner` (NP).

Even if the doctor has already done a regular physical exam, he or she may order special tests or ask different questions. SOME BEHAVIORAL PROBLEMS CAN BE CAUSED BY PHYSICAL CONDITIONS OR SIDE EFFECTS OF OTHER MEDICATIONS. If that's the case, your doctor may want to refer you to a **medical specialist.** If not, the physician may refer you to a **behavioral health specialist.** If your child doesn't seem to be developing certain types of skills in the same way as most children of the same age, the doctor may also refer you to a **developmental health specialist.** Some of these specialties are described on the next page.

Be sure to bring this physical examination record to any specialists who evaluate or treat your child. They may not do full examinations themselves. This information is also important when you fill out `health history` forms, which you will often need to do each time you visit a new person. (On page 22 is a short health history form you can use to store information for easy reference each time you have to fill out a new form. This will save a lot of time and stress!)

2 Getting Prepared
CONTINUED

Good Questions

When you don't understand, keep asking! It will save you (and the professional) a lot of trouble and confusion. Health professionals can be very rushed — but an informed parent is the best partner. Most will respect a parent more for asking questions.

In some rural counties and other areas that are short on behavioral health professionals, the pediatrician or other primary care doctor may prescribe medications for behavioral health issues. (Some primary care doctors and pediatricians also have special training in behavioral health issues.)

In some cases, a doctor may order a blood test or other procedure (such as an MRI) to find out if a medical condition is causing your child's behavior. However, it is important to know that no current medical test can determine for sure that your child has depression, ADHD (Attention Deficit Hyperactivity Disorder), anxiety, or any other behavioral disorder. Professionals must rely on what they observe and what they hear from others in order to make a diagnosis.

NOTE: If your child begins treatment with a psychiatrist or other behavioral health specialist, be sure to keep the primary care doctor informed and involved. For example, certain medications for ADHD or mood disorders can affect a child's weight or risk for diseases such as diabetes. If so, your primary care doctor can work with you on a plan to prevent or treat such conditions before they become big problems for your child.

Discuss the matter with your child's **classroom teacher or school counselor**, too. They may notice a lot of behaviors you don't see at home. They can also give you a better idea of how your child is acting or developing compared to other children of that age. (See more in Chapter 5, "The Classroom-Treatment Connection.")

Mental health centers often have a series of steps for evaluating and treating mental health problems. In many cases, you'll see a number of different professionals and may not see the same people at your next appointment. If there is anything you don't understand, **ASK TO HAVE THE PROCESS EXPLAINED TO YOU.**

The best way to get the information you need is to ask questions that begin with **Who…? What…? When…? Where…? Why….? How…?** and **Can you explain…?**

For example, you might ask:
- **Who** will we need to see next?
- **What** will happen next?
- **Where** will this happen?
- **When** can we expect this to happen?
- **How** can I contact you or that person?
- **Why** is my child seeing this specialist?
- **Can you explain** how this process works?

On the next page you'll find some descriptions of medical, behavioral, and developmental specialists.

Know Your Support Staff

Receptionists, physicians' assistants, administrators, technicians, and **nurses** *can be a great source of information about how things work in a professional's office or clinic. Take time to notice them, learn their names, and ask for their advice.*

Medical, behavioral, and developmental health specialists who may evaluate your child include:

MEDICAL DOCTORS AND NURSES who can prescribe medications:

Psychiatrist: A medical doctor who is trained to evaluate and treat your child's behavior, primarily by prescribing medications. A psychiatrist has the most formal training in behavioral health but may spend the least amount of time with you and your child during treatment. A psychiatrist who specializes in how medications work and are prescribed is called a **"psychopharmacologist."**

Behavioral/Developmental Pediatrician: Combines physical, psychological, and developmental evaluation as well as treatment.

Neurologist: Medical doctor who specializes in how the brain functions physically and chemically.

Licensed Psychiatric Nurse Practitioner: Assists in or performs clinical evaluations, designs treatment plans, and may provide counseling, medication management, or other treatment.

MENTAL HEALTH PROFESSIONALS who give evaluation or treatment but do not prescribe medications:

Clinical Psychologist: Licensed by the state to evaluate your child's behavioral health and academic performance. May also provide psychotherapy, a form of counseling that is commonly known as "talk therapy" but may include other kinds of one-on-one or group treatment.

School Psychologist: Employed by the school system to do various evaluations. May provide a "psycho-educational" evaluation to determine the child's skills and ability to learn compared with other children of the same age. A psycho-educational evaluation does not diagnose mental illness. However, it may be used to determine a child's need for special school services.

Licensed Clinical Social Worker: Licensed by the state to provide one-on-one or group therapy.

Case Manager: Helps to coordinate services for a family and make referrals for behavioral health care as well as other community resources (such as food, housing, clothing, etc.).

2 Getting Prepared
CONTINUED

Learn More About Developmental Issues

The University of Michigan Health Systems website on developmental delays offers clear, simple definitions and advice for parents. Go to http://www.med.umich.edu/1libr/yourchild/

One of the most visited children's health sites is www.kidshealth.org, from the Nemours Foundation's Center for Children's Health Media. Separate sites allow younger children and teens to browse for health information.

Counseling and Evaluation Professionals: Some professionals (including those listed above) may have other titles, such as Licensed Psychological Examiner, Licensed Marriage and Family Therapist, or Licensed Professional Counselor. Feel free to ask questions about the training and state license of your child's therapist to gain a better understanding of his or her background. (The professional usually shows certificates on his or her office wall. The state requires that a copy of the professional's state license must be posted in the building where he or she works.)

DEVELOPMENTAL SPECIALISTS who may evaluate or treat your child:

Speech Language Pathologist: Evaluates and treats the way a child understands and uses communication. This includes spoken language plus "non-verbal" signals such as eye contact and body language. The SLP deals with how sounds are pronounced ("articulation") and voice quality ("hoarseness, pitch"). The SLP also studies "social language" (ability to understand social cues, talk back and forth with someone, or solve problems through communication). May do therapy for oral skills such as feeding, or academic skills such as reading.

Occupational Therapist: Evaluates and treats problems with "fine motor skills" (use of the small muscles of the body, such as those in fingers), daily living skills (for example, dressing), and vocational skills, such as following a set of instructions. An OT may evaluate and treat "sensory integration" problems (how a person's brain understands and responds to signals from the five senses).

Physical Therapist: Evaluates and treats problems with gross motor skills (use of large muscles of the body such as those in arms and legs). The PT may use massage, movement, and special equipment to train the body or help a person adapt to disabilities.

Audiologist: Evaluates the way sounds are heard or understood by the brain. This person may evaluate how loud a sound needs to be or whether the brain "reads" that sound correctly.

Behavior Analyst: Provides evaluation of behavior problems to determine why they occur. Develops a plan to change the behavior or adapt the environment. This professional sometimes uses a method called Applied Behavioral Analysis (ABA).

Special Education Teacher: Licensed to teach children with disabilities in school.

Getting Ready for An Intake Interview

An ⟦intake interview⟧ is the first appointment with a new health professional or agency. At this appointment, you will be asked to give information about your child and discuss his or her symptoms. ⟦Symptoms⟧ are signs of disease that may include physical changes, thoughts, feelings, and behaviors.

Learning how to identify symptoms clearly is important for many reasons. First, the appointment time goes by very quickly, so you want to make the most of the time you have. Second, the behavior your child shows during an office visit may be very different from the way he or she acts at home. It will help the professional if you can describe normal home behavior. Third, you will probably have to fill out a questionnaire that includes this same information. (Sometimes the professional will ask you questions from a list and will write down the answers for you.)

Most parents end up repeating this same "symptom story" to different professionals on the team. The method described below can help boil it down to the basics.

Five Steps to Describing the "Symptom Story"

On the next few pages you will find a five-step process to help you describe medical, behavioral, and developmental symptoms during an intake interview. The health professional needs to know about all three areas because everything in your child's body is connected. For example, certain behavior symptoms can be signs of thyroid disease, a medical condition. Certain physical ailments, such as frequent headaches and stomachaches, may be symptoms of a mood disorder. A child who gets very upset or irritable in noisy places may have a developmental problem that needs special therapy. In each case, finding the root cause or causes will help the child to get better treatment.

Step One: List Medical (Physical) Symptoms
Step Two: List Behavioral Symptoms
Step Three: Consider Your Child's Developmental Profile
Step Four: Identify the Top Concerns
Step Five: Sum Up the Symptoms

Learn More

The National Institute for Mental Health offers a useful booklet on what to do if you suspect your child has a behavioral health issue. Go to http://www.nimh.nih.gov/health/publications.

The homepage includes a summary of the most common childhood mental disorders. It describes the treatments and medications most often used, and it answers frequently asked questions. You can download the entire booklet or order it by mail.

Step One: List Medical (Physical) Symptoms

Check the symptoms that have occurred "Never, Occasionally, Often, or Very Often" in the last six months.

	Never	Occasionally	Often	Very Often
1. Headaches				
2. Stomachaches				
3. Fever				
4. Dizziness				
5. Tires easily				
6. Sleeps much more than usual				
7. Sleeps less or complains of being unable to sleep				
8. Low energy				
9. Unexplained rashes				
10. Recent weight gain				
11. Recent weight loss				
12. Vision problems				
13. Hearing problems				
14. Ear infections				
Other Ailments:				

SUICIDE AND VIOLENCE RISK

If your child shows any of these signs:
- Sudden change in personality
- Gives away many favorite possessions
- Talks of wanting to die or "disappear"
- Takes unusual risks or shows reckless behavior
- Threatens suicide or violence
- Talks of family or others being "better off without me"
- Has a sudden and frequent interest in death or methods of dying
- Collects objects that may cause harm to self or others,

TAKE IT SERIOUSLY. DO NOT DELAY. Seek immediate help from your doctor. In a crisis situation, call your local Specialized Crisis Services phone number. If you can't find this number, call the nearest psychiatric hospital for information, or call 911. Staff will come help you determine if your child needs emergency care.

See Chapter 7 for more on "Coping with Crisis."

Step Two: List Behavioral Symptoms

Check the symptoms that have occurred "Never, Occasionally, Often, or Very Often" in the last six months. At the bottom of page 18, add any other symptoms not on this list.

	Never	Occasionally	Often	Very Often
1. Often loses personal items (ex. clothes, textbooks).				
2. Doesn't pay attention to details on homework.				
3. Has trouble paying attention to jobs or chores at home.				
4. Has trouble getting organized to do schoolwork.				
5. Doesn't play with other children.				
6. Pulls out hair from head or body.				
7. Lines up objects rather than playing with them.				
8. Lectures children on a high-interest topic even when they seem uninterested.				
9. Has trouble sharing with other children.				
10. Has trouble playing quiet activities.				
11. Has trouble changing from one activity to another.				
12. Gets overexcited or overstressed, even at fun occasions (e.g. birthday parties).				
13. Grades have dropped a lot recently.				
14. Teachers report more "acting out" behavior.				
15. Teachers report child seems more "sad" or "lost" lately.				
16. Has tantrums or shows unusually angry behavior when other children win at games.				
17. Becomes giddy or irritable for no apparent reason; a short time later is quiet and sad.				
18. Eats very little in order to lose weight, even though already thin.				
19. Recently shows little interest in spending time with friends.				
20. Fights with other children.				
21. Starts many projects without finishing them.				
22. Can't seem to sit still even when trying to do so.				
23. Is fearful of going to school.				
24. Is easily frustrated.				
25. Has temper tantrums.				
26. Gets very anxious or worries a lot.				
27. Has fixed "rituals" that he/she needs to do to in order to feel okay.				
28. Destroys objects.				
29. Has deliberately set fires.				
30. Has hurt others on purpose.				
31. Deliberately destroys property of others.				
32. Has used a weapon that can cause serious harm.				
33. Has run away from home overnight.				
34. Has stayed out at night without permission.				

Behavioral Symptoms, continued

	Never	Occasionally	Often	Very Often
35. Says he/she feels worthless or inferior.				
36. Says, "no one loves me."				
37. Has committed a crime.				
38. Feels guilty, thinks problems are "all my fault."				
39. Seems sad, lonely, or depressed.				
40. Is cruel to animals.				
41. Is physically cruel to others.				
42. Has trouble making friends.				
43. Has trouble keeping friends.				
44. Gets embarrassed very easily.				
45. Seems unusually shy with others.				
46. Is afraid to try new things due to fear of making a mistake.				
47. Lies to or "cons" others to get out of trouble, avoid things, or get things.				
48. Fidgets with hands or feet.				
49. Leaves seat at school or elsewhere when supposed to stay seated.				
50. Has difficulty waiting his or her turn.				
51. Interrupts others' conversations.				
52. Bullies or threatens others.				
53. Is angry and resentful.				
54. Acts on impulse.				
55. Defies adults or refuses to go along with requests and rules, despite possibility of punishment.				
56. Talks too much or too rapidly.				
57. Is "touchy" or easily annoyed by others.				
58. Blames others for his/her mistakes or behavior.				
59. Doesn't seem to listen when spoken to directly.				
60. Doesn't like to be touched.				
61. Skips school without permission.				
62. Has stolen valuable things.				
63. Argues with those in authority.				

Other symptoms:

Sources: American Academy of Pediatrics, North Carolina Center for Children's Healthcare Improvement, National Initiative for Children's Healthcare Quality, NICHQ Vanderbilt Assessment Scale–Parent Informant. In: *Caring for Children with ADHD: A Resource Toolkit for Clinicians.* Elk Grove Village, IL; American Academy of Pediatrics; 2005. Additional source: "Pediatric Symptom Checklist" by Michael Jellinek, MD, and Michael Murphy, EdD, Massachusetts General Hospital, Boston, MA. Additional material from ADHD checklist by Linda Zweifel, Director of Programs, NAMI Montgomery County, Texas; adapted with permission from author.

Step Three:
Consider Your Child's Developmental Profile

Each child has a unique **"developmental profile."** This means the way he or she performs certain functions compared to a typical child of that age. Children develop at different speeds, but most gain certain skills at roughly the same time. When this doesn't happen, it may affect behavior. Development differences don't always mean your child has another disorder. However, the profile can help your team design a treatment plan that works best. Some "developmental profile" terms you may hear include:

Sensory Processing: How does the child learn best—by seeing, hearing, smelling, tasting, or touching?

_____

Sensory Modulation: Does he/she seem to react too much or not enough to sounds, touch, or light? Do rough clothing, new shoes, or shirt tags make him/her unable to concentrate? Does he/she avoid certain "normal" sensations or seek them out? _____

_____

Communication: When did your child begin to babble? Speak in words? String words into simple sentences? Does your child (above age 2) use back-and-forth talk with others? Use conversation to ask for things and information? _____

_____

Social Skills: Is your child naturally affectionate or reserved? Does he/she form attachments easily? Get along in groups of same-age children? Seem to understand and be able to play games with rules? Understand what others are feeling and signaling by their actions? Does he/she seem to understand body language? _____

_____

Emotional Modulation: How well does the child handle changing emotions and moods? Is he/she generally happy and calm or often agitated and irritable? Easily affected by noisy or hectic situations? How well does he/she put up with frustration? Can he/she calm herself independently after getting upset?

_____

Cognitive Ability: How easily does your child learn things compared to others his/her age? What types of learning (for example, numbers and math, language or reading) seem hardest for him/her?

_____

_____

Motor Skills and Planning: How well does the child move "in space" compared to other children of the same age? How well does he/she run? Does he/she have trouble with skills such as shoe-tying or zipping a coat? Can he/she carry out tasks that include several steps? _____

_____

Attention: Can the child focus easily on "fun" activities? Activities that are assigned by others? Work independently? Is it hard to get his/her attention? Is he/she easily distracted? Does he/she seem to pay attention to people and things around him/her? _____

_____

Step Four: Identify the Top Concerns

Go back to your three lists and put checkmarks next to the TOP FIVE symptoms that concern you most. These are the things that interfere most with the child's home, school, family, or social life. You may also want to look back at the concerns you listed on page 7. Knowing which symptoms cause the greatest concern can help your team figure out where to start.

Step Five: Sum Up the Symptoms

In this final step, describe the Top Five symptoms briefly IN YOUR OWN WORDS. (For example: "Always tired. Lies in bed after school every day for the last month.") Try to note where and when the troubling behavior shows up. Is it at family gatherings or at unstructured "hang out" time with peers? Does it happen at certain seasons? Certain times of day, such as bedtime? Does it happen more in public places or during school activities? How long has this behavior gone on?

Make a note if the behavior happened during or after a certain event, such as a change at school or a loss in your child's personal life. It is important to be frank about changes in your own life (such as a divorce or loss of a job) that may affect your child's emotions, behavior, or daily routine.

	When	Where	How Long
Symptom 1:			
Symptom 2:			
Symptom 3:			
Symptom 4:			
Symptom 5:			

Other issues, comments, or questions:

Make at least two copies of these worksheets and file in your binder under "Doctors and Clinicians" (see the next page). Keep one copy and give the other to the doctor at the time of your appointment. *Brief* written information or questions in your own words can be very useful at any appointment. Make sure the professional looks at the **last sheet** (your top five concerns). This list can help you and the professional have a more useful conversation. Also, the doctor or clinician can put this parent report into the child's file for future reference. **Providing information in an organized way tends to make professionals treat parents as equal partners. This will be very important as treatment goes on!**

Keeping Your Child's Records

A 2-inch, 3-ring binder is the best way to keep paperwork organized and available when you go to appointments or make phone calls to professionals. Put a cheap, three-hole-punched calendar (often available at supermarkets and pharmacies) in the front to record appointments. Add this book to your binder. You can use the worksheets on the next pages to keep many important records. Label the binder with the month and year you started it.

Add five tabbed dividers labeled "personal data," "doctor visits," "medications," "evaluations," "school," and "insurance and social agencies." In the personal data section, include a copy of your child's insurance card and Social Security card or number. Add a few sheets of filler paper to each section in case you need to make notes. Some parents like to put the child's photo on the inside front cover.

You may think of more categories and ways to organize later. DO IT YOUR WAY and you'll be more likely to keep using it. It's best to use this binder for a year, file it away on the shelf, and then start a new notebook. That way, you'll have an easy way to refer back over the years.

Your Child's Health History

Before seeing a new specialist, you will usually be asked to fill out a health history form. These forms are used to describe the child's personal information (such as address, date of birth, and Social Security number). It will ask about insurance coverage, a list of developmental milestones (such as age of sitting up, walking, talking in sentences, etc.), physical health, medications, and symptoms. Questions about you, your spouse, or other children in the home may also be included.

It can be very nerve-wracking to fill out this form in 10 or 15 minutes while sitting in a crowded waiting room with a youngster who may need extra attention! Whenever possible, try to have this form mailed to you before the appointment so that you can fill it in on your own time. Feel free to add as many extra sheets as you need, because the space on the form is usually pretty tight. It can help to attach a copy of the child's latest physical examination and your list of the child's behavioral symptoms. Write "See attached summaries" on parts of the form. Write as neatly as possible.

Zip It Up

You may want to add a zipper pouch in the front to keep a pen, pencil, small hole punch, envelopes, stamps and sticky notes. You can also use it to store small items such as prescriptions, appointment cards, or business cards from professionals.

2 Getting Prepared
CONTINUED

Get a Head Start!

Use the next three pages to keep basic data. You can refer to it each time you have to fill out a new set of forms. Each clinician's form will be different, but almost all will ask for the information on these pages.

Fill this form out in pencil so you can update when necessary—or write on a copy and file in your binder. You can also keep this record on your computer using the CD you can purchase at www.meltonhillmedia.com.

Health History for _____
(Name of child)

Date _____

Last name _____

First name _____ Middle name _____

Home address _____
_____

Male ___ Female ___ Birth Date _____ Current Age _____

Where born (city, state, and country) _____

Social Security number _____

Year in school _____ Name of school _____

Language(s) child speaks at home _____

Medical History

Any troubles during pregnancy or birth (examples: jaundice, premature birth):
_____

Physical diseases. Conditions or injuries at the present time (examples: juvenile diabetes, anemia):

What: _____ How long: _____
What: _____ How long: _____
What: _____ How long: _____

Physical diseases. Conditions or injuries in the past, with dates if you know them (examples: seizures, frequent ear infections):

What: _____ Began when: _____
What: _____ Began when: _____
What: _____ Began when: _____

Alcohol, tobacco, or illegal drug use (see note on page 24):

Now: _____
_____

In the past (include when used): _____
_____

Behavioral health issues already diagnosed (example: depression):

Diagnosis: _____ When diagnosed: _____
Any other diagnosis: _____ When diagnosed: _____

Current prescription drugs taken (with dosage):

What: _____ For: _____
What: _____ For: _____
What: _____ For: _____

Non-prescription drugs taken (include vitamins, herbs, supplements and over-the-counter drugs such as cold medicines or pain relievers):
_____

Allergies: _____

Family Medical History

Health professionals often ask about illnesses in close family members. This is because genetic traits (physical and mental qualities you are born with) can lead to certain illnesses that run in families. Knowing a particular illness has occurred in a close relative may help a doctor determine what's happening to your child. In some cases, a medication that is used to treat a mental illness in one family member may have a better chance to be successful with another family member.

Remember: The genetic traits your child inherited are nobody's fault and nothing that anyone can control. These are just pieces of information that help fill in the picture. If you have concerns about who will be able to see your personal information, discuss this with the doctor or other professional who evaluates your child.

Health History, continued

Drug reactions: _____

Date of last physical exam: _____

Date of last eye exam: _____

Date of last hearing exam: _____

Last dental visit: _____

Immunization ("shot") record. Show latest date given (or get a copy of this record from the child's primary care doctor and keep it with the health history form).

DTaP (Diptheria, tetanus, and acellular pertussis): _____

Hepatitis A: _____

Hepatitis B: _____

Hepatitis C (if given): _____

Hib (Influenza vaccine, type b): _____

IPV (Inactive poliovirus): _____

MMR (Measles, mumps, rubella): _____

PCV (Pneumonia vaccine): _____

Td (Tetanus and diphtheria, if given separately from above): _____

Social History

Mother's Name: _____

Date of Birth: _____ Age: _____ SSN: _____

Living or deceased: _____

Address: _____

_____

Name and address of mother's employer: _____

_____

Father's Name: _____

Date of Birth: _____ Age: _____ SSN: _____

Living or deceased: _____

Address: _____

_____

Name and address of father's employer: _____

_____

Birth parents' names, if different: _____

Child lives with (name and relationship to child): _____

Is the child adopted? _____   In foster care? _____

At what age was the child placed? _____

Parents' marital status:

Married __ Divorced __ When _____ Separated __ When _____

2 Getting Prepared
CONTINUED

Alcohol, Drug Abuse, and Other Behaviors

It is very important that professionals who work with your child know about anything that can affect your child's health, behavior, and emotions. That means knowing about family alcohol and drug abuse, sexual abuse, and any unusual family behaviors or traumas *(very negative bad events such as a death, injury, or divorce) that your child has experienced.*

In most cases, the professional is required to keep this information confidential *(not telling the police, your employer, or others not involved in the child's treatment) unless the situation will cause a major risk to the child or others.* **There are exceptions to this rule.**

If you have any questions, talk to the professional about how the information will be used. If you aren't comfortable listing the information on the forms in this book, write it down in a safe place and don't forget to share it with the professional.

Health History, continued

Number and ages of child's siblings (brothers and sisters): _____
_____

How many live with child? _____

Relatives or others living with child: _____
_____

Numbers and ages of siblings not living with child (including step-siblings):
_____
_____
_____
_____

Describe any important life events in the past that affect your child's physical or behavioral health (example: family divorce, major move, tragedy/trauma):
_____
_____
_____
_____

Family Health History

Describe any medical, behavioral, or mental health diagnoses in parents, grandparents, or siblings: _____
_____
_____
_____

Describe any unusual, "weird," or negative behavior in close family members. (Example: older brother and father often have sudden rages.) INCLUDE ALCOHOL AND ILLEGAL DRUG USE. _____
_____
_____
_____
_____

Developmental History

At about what age did the child:

Roll over without help _____   Sit up without support _____

Crawl _____ Walk _____   Eat solid foods _____

Feed self with spoon _____   Babble _____

Point to objects _____   Use single words _____

Use a string of three words _____   Speak in sentences _____

Developmental Milestones

It can be hard to remember when a child did certain things. Sometimes it helps to look at family pictures. This record may also be in your primary care doctor's files. You may need to compare notes with others in the family. That's why it's better to gather this information ahead of time.

Health History, continued

How often does the child get regular exercise? _____

What kind(s) of exercise or sports? _____

Any unusual diet or feeding problems? _____

Other comments about physical, mental, or developmental health (look back at "Your Child's Developmental Profile" on page 19, for other information to include): _____

_____
_____
_____
_____
_____
_____
_____

Doctors, Therapists, and Other Professionals

(To develop a full list of professional contacts, use the worksheet on page 41.)

Primary Care Doctor or Pediatrician:

Name, address, and phone number: _____

_____
_____

Specialists (Name, specialty, address, phone number):

1. _____
_____

2. _____
_____

3. _____
_____

4. _____
_____

Case Manager (name, organization, phone number):

Name: _____

Organization: _____

Contact phone number: _____

Health Insurance

Plan: _____

Group Policy number: _____

Your child's ID #: _____

Customer Service or information phone number: _____

2 Getting Prepared
CONTINUED

Straight Talk

Straight Talk About Psychological Testing for Kids by Ellen Braaten, PhD and Gretchen Felopulos, PhD (The Guilford Press, New York, 2004) explains how to know if your child needs testing. It describes what the tests measure, and what all those number scores mean. It also helps you understand the common technical language used in evaluation reports. Easy to use and well written!

Making Sense of Reports and Evaluations

The professional who evaluates your child (usually a psychologist or social worker) is sometimes called a clinician. This person may use one or more tests (standardized assessment tools or test batteries) to help determine your child's needs. There are many different types of tests, and in most cases the clinician must get your written permission to give the test to your child.

Some questions to ask:
1. **What** is the name of the test?
2. **Why** is my child being given this test?
3. **What** kinds of information will this test provide?
4. **When** will this test be given?
5. **How** long will the test take?
6. **Who** will administer (give) the test to my child?
7. **When** will I receive the results of this test?

These are some common types of tests used to evaluate children with behavioral health issues:

Cognitive and Adaptive: These types of tests are used to measure the way a child's brain works in terms of intelligence, memory, life skills, attention, use of language, and ways of learning. Some often-used tests in this category include the Woodcock-Johnson, WISC, and Vineland Scales of Adaptive Behavior.

Psychological Evaluation: This type of test explores a child's emotional health, social abilities, behavior, and personality. You will usually be asked to fill out a questionnaire about the behavior you see at home. A teacher may also be asked to fill out such a form. (Many of the common symptoms listed on pages 17-18 would appear on this kind of questionnaire.) Some tests in this category include sentence-completion tests, the Children's Depression Inventory, or the Behavioral Assessment System for Children (BASC).

Developmental Evaluation: This kind of test measures a young child's development level compared to same-age children. It measures some of the development areas mentioned on page 19. One common test is the Bayley Scales of Infant Development.

Educational (or Psycho-educational) Evaluation: Most often given by the school psychologist, these tests measure intelligence, academic skills, and academic abilities (how the child can and does perform in school compared to others the same age). A psycho-educational evaluation does not diagnose mental illness. School psychologists often use the Woodcock-Johnson, WISC, and Vineland as well as academic achievement tests. They may also do psychological and developmental evaluations using other types of tests mentioned above. See Chapter 5 for more on school testing.

More About Professional Titles

The organizations that give health and social services are often called providers. Some providers have private practices that employ only one or a few professionals. Some private practices are attached to hospitals or clinics. A larger organization that gives behavioral health services may be called a CMHC (Community Mental Health Center), a CMHO (Community Mental Health Organization), or CMHA (Community Mental Health Agency). These organizations may employ many psychiatrists, psychologists, social workers, case managers, and support staff. In this book, the words "professionals" and "providers" mean people that provide services. Clinician means someone who evaluates your child and may later provide therapy. A therapist is a psychologist (PhD or PsyD), social worker (LCSW), or licensed counselor who provides so-called "talk therapy." (Such therapy may also involve other methods, such as playing games or doing activities with your child.)

Choosing Someone to Evaluate Your Child

A primary care provider may refer your child to a specific doctor, clinic, or other specialist. The school may suggest that you look for a specialist. Maybe you are concerned about a problem and decide to look for help on your own. You may have to pick someone from the list of providers in your network. In any case, the choice of a clinician is up to YOU. How do you pick the right person? There are no simple answers. **(Note: If you have state-funded (public) health insurance, you may not need a referral from your PCP. However, you should always discuss this with the primary care doctor first, to rule out other medical problems.)**

Many parents are bothered by the thought of going to someone who will ask them lots of personal questions. "You feel as if somebody's opening your door, walking into your house, and looking in your closets," says Ronda Redden Reitz, a psychotherapist who often evaluates children. "A parent can't help feeling judged somehow."

It's easy to understand that feeling. This person will ask a lot of questions about your family life. The way you and your child behave toward one another will be observed. The evaluator forms an opinion of your situation from the way you talk to your child, fill out forms, and answer questions. "Often the evaluation starts while you are still sitting in the waiting room," Redden Reitz adds.

Remember that you also have the right to observe and evaluate the professional who will deal with your child. You are seeking help because you need to solve a problem. You can do that best when you feel comfortable giving someone all the information necessary. That means you need someone who knows how to listen. The best clinician will gather the facts and not jump to conclusions.

Doc Talk

The American Medical Association's Guide to Talking to Your Doctor (Angela Perry, MD, Medical Editor, John Wiley & Sons, Inc., New York, 2001) *offers clear, basic tips on exchanging information with a doctor. Included are chapters on choosing a doctor, taking children to the doctor, and dealing with special situations such as emergencies. The behavioral health parts of the book are limited, but the general health checklists are very useful. A long glossary in the back provides clear descriptions of medical specialties and common diseases.*

2 Getting Prepared
CONTINUED

SED: How It Adds Up

According to federal guidelines, a child with SED (Serious Emotional Disturbance) has a diagnosed mental, behavioral, or emotional disorder that lasts long enough and is severe enough to interfere with functioning in family, school, or community activities.

One in ten children (ten percent) *is affected by Serious Emotional Disturbance (SED) at some time.*

At least fifty percent of children *in state custody have mental health problems.*

Two-thirds of young people with mental health problems *are not getting the help they need.*

Sources: Vanderbilt University Center for Mental Health Policy/Kids Count 2002; Surgeon General's Report on Children's Mental Health, 2000; and Center for Mental Health Services. Updated SED data from: Tennessee Commission on Children and Youth, 2004. Statistics courtesy of Tennessee Voices for Children Parent Leadership Training.

The most well known or recommended person in town may not be right for you or your child. You have to trust your gut instinct. You have to notice things like body language that may hint about whether the clinician and your child will get along. Some people like to bring a relative or trusted friend along to the first appointment. That way, you have an independent view and someone to take notes on what was said.

If you are considering a clinician who has a private practice, try to talk to this person on the phone first. Ask questions such as:

1. How long have you been in practice?
2. How much of your practice is with children?
3. What type of degree do you have?
4. Do you have experience in working with school systems to get services? Would you be willing to go to a school meeting if necessary?
5. My child seems to have (explain problem very briefly). How many children have you seen with this type of problem?
6. Can you please explain what the steps of the evaluation will be? Will you wish to see me separately before you see my child?
7. What sorts of tests do you generally use?
8. What do you charge?
9. Do you file insurance paperwork? What is your procedure for payment?
10. Can I contact you between appointments if necessary? How do you prefer to be contacted between visits?

Tips for a First Visit

When you see a provider for the first time, ask the same questions. Pay attention to small cues that could mean a lot. A good clinician will usually begin by asking something like "Why are you here?" He or she will clearly explain methods for working together, payment arrangements, and what your role in treatment will be. (For example, the clinician might say, "After I meet with your child for about three weeks, I'll want us to get together and review the treatment plan.")

The person may want to meet with your child a few times before deciding what, if any, tests to use. If so, you should be given some idea of when to expect this decision. If the child is a teen, the clinician may want to keep some parts of their therapy discussions confidential (not telling you). The clinician may do this to build up more trust so the child will be frank and honest in discussions. If that's the case, you should be told clearly in the beginning in order to give your consent.

Code Words

Clinical evaluation reports often include certain terms that are "shorthand" for things one professional tells another. It might include sentences like "Jane was neatly groomed and appropriately dressed for the season." This means the child seems to be well cared-for.

Tip: *If, despite your best efforts, your child shows up at the evaluation very messy, in shoes full of holes or wearing shorts on a freezing day, explain to the evaluator why. ("I know it looks strange, but wearing long pants makes him have a meltdown.") If the hot water failed that morning and nobody could take a shower, explain this. Don't be embarrassed, just frank. Remember, the clinician isn't a mind-reader. He or she knows your child's behavior is difficult for you. Full information will only help.*

You should discuss exactly what kinds of information will and will not be shared.

Pay attention to the person's manner and the office environment. Does the clinician make you and your child feel comfortable? Do you feel your concerns are being heard? If the child has to wait somewhere while you speak to the person privately, is that space safe and comfortable? What does your child think?

If your child receives services from a large agency, one person may evaluate your child, and a different person may give therapy. Others (such as a nurse or psychiatrist) may be in charge of medication management. YOU STILL HAVE A CHOICE. If one of these persons doesn't seem right to you, you can request someone else. Talk to your case manager if you don't know how to do this. If necessary, ask an administrator in the clinic. Unfortunately, in some small cities and rural areas there aren't many clinicians, therapists, or psychiatrists. If you really don't think any of the professionals seem right for your child, find out whether it's practical to go to a larger city.

Of course, you may need to see the person for more than one visit before you make any judgment. People don't always "click" right away. For more information about this topic, see Chapter 3 on "Working with the Team."

Understanding the Treatment Plan

Once the evaluation process is complete, the clinician will meet with you to develop a **treatment plan.** This can take a number of different forms. In some cases, there will be a written report, sometimes called a "clinical evaluation report" or "clinical assessment report." This report will state the reason your child was referred, sum up the child's health history, explain test results, and make recommendations for treatment.

Always be sure the evaluator gives you a copy of any report or treatment plan that concerns your child. Often the clinician will go over a "draft" report so you can pick out any errors or things you disagree about. **READ THE REPORT CAREFULLY. Ask about any results or terms you don't understand.** Pay careful attention to anything in the report about your child's past medications, illnesses, or your family history. Mark your corrections clearly on your copy and file in your binder. Ask when you can expect to receive a final copy of this report. When you receive it, make sure the corrections were made. Save this copy. If you don't receive it when promised, ask again and keep asking. **It's very important to have an accurate evaluation report because it becomes part of your child's record. It will be used by other professionals who treat your child.**

2 Getting Prepared
CONTINUED

En Su Lengua

La mayoría de las organizaciones grandes de salud harán el intento de traducir en su idioma (POR ESCRITO) el plan de tratamiento, si usted no lee inglés adecuadamente. Solicite este servicio si lo necesita. Es importante que usted entienda el plan para que pueda consentir al mismo y se pueda involucrar debidamente.

Treatment Plan Forms

Large clinics, hospitals, and CMHAs often use a standard form for the treatment plan. Most plans contain this type of information:

STATEMENT OF THE PROBLEM: This part should describe the problem or problems in plain words. It may also include the diagnosis.

Example: "John is often physically aggressive to children at school. At home, John is observed to cycle rapidly between extreme irritation and sadness. Symptoms get worse in winter. Diagnosis: Bipolar disorder with rapid cycling and Seasonal Affective Disorder."

LONG-TERM GOALS: This is how the team pictures a good outcome of treatment.

Example: "John will learn and practice successful methods for managing anger without aggression. John's moods will be stable enough throughout the year to allow functional school, home, and social activity."

SHORT-TERM GOALS: These are specific goals the team will work on immediately. If possible, there should be some way to measure whether progress toward these goals is being made. It should include a date to review whether the plan is working.

Example: "John will decrease physical attacks on children to less than one per week. John will show increased mood stability over a period of one month. Review progress with parent after one month from start of treatment." (Remember: These are goals, not promises. It's hard to predict whether or how soon a person's behavior will change.)

INTERVENTION PLAN: These are actions people on the team will take to help your child reach the goals. An intervention plan should always list what will be done, who will do it, and how often actions will happen. It should list a start date and an estimated date to complete or review the actions. *The plan should also include what you and other family members will do.*

Example:
(1) "Medications to be prescribed by Doctor A for aggression and mood stability. Weekly medication management by Nurse B until John is stable for one month. Review medication as needed.
(2) Psychotherapy sessions with MSW Therapist C twice weekly.
(3) Family therapy session with C every two weeks.
(4) Team meeting with parents in one month or sooner if needed."

CRISIS PLAN: If your child's condition poses a threat to himself, the family, or others, this part should describe what steps will be taken if things get a lot worse. The plan should tell you whom to contact first (such as the local Mental Health Crisis or Specialized Crisis Services number) and which hospital will accept your child in a crisis. It should also tell you who will be the contact person on the team to give you advice, and who will communicate with the hospital. Sometimes this plan is put on another form. Make sure it includes all necessary phone numbers.

OTHER INFORMATION AND NEEDS: If your child has special needs that affect the plan (such as a medical condition or disability), this should be stated on the treatment plan.

You and all members of the treatment team who will provide these services should sign this plan. If you don't agree, state what the problems are and discuss them. Ask about alternatives. **Remember to put a copy of this treatment plan in your binder.**

Sometimes a clinician will prefer to see your child for a while before developing a treatment plan. Some professionals (especially those in private practice) don't use written treatment plans. This may be okay. You have to judge whether it's comfortable for you. However, getting a plan on paper ensures there are fewer misunderstandings. It provides a way to see if progress is being made. It includes estimated times to review and change treatment. You can send copies to your primary care provider and school to keep them informed.

If your clinician or case manager doesn't offer any form of treatment plan, ask why not. If you would prefer to have one, say so. A good team member will be willing to work with you.

Getting Medication Facts

If medication is part of your child's treatment plan, here are some questions you might ask the doctor or nurse:

1. How will this medication help my child?
2. How commonly is the medication used in children of this age?
3. How much experience do you personally have with prescribing this medication for children?
4. Is this a brand-name medication? Is it available in a less expensive generic version?
5. What is the name of the generic version? Can we use it?
6. Can we switch between brands or between the generic and the brand-name medicine?
7. What is the dosage? Is it likely to change during the time my child is getting used to it? Will my child need a different dose as she grows?
8. What if my child can't swallow a pill or capsule? Is it available in chewable or liquid form?
9. How many times a day must the medicine be taken? What time of day? Does it need to be taken with food?
10. How long will my child have to take this medication?

Fast Facts for Families

*The American Academy of Child & Adolescent Psychiatry answers common questions about medications in its **"Facts for Families"** series at www.aacap.org. The series also includes a useful information sheet on issues facing military families.*

Need advice about toddler toilet training? Safe teen dating? Summer planning for an ADHD child? The "Frequently Asked Questions" page on the website of New York University Child Study Center is a fast way to find links to solid advice on a behavior topic. Go to www.aboutourkids.org.

2 Getting Prepared
CONTINUED

Medline Plus

The website www.medlineplus.org, a service of the National Library of Medicine and the National Institutes of Health, covers hundreds of health topics and describes a huge number of medications. You'll find plain-spoken information about drug interactions and current warnings. Also included is an encyclopedia of medical terms and links to many other useful sites.

The PDR website provides drug information for families at www.pdrhealth.com.

11. Who will monitor (keep track of) my child's medications?
12. Will my child need any laboratory tests with this medication? If so, how often?
13. Does my child need to avoid any foods when taking this medication?
14. What are possible side effects? Which ones are most likely?
15. What side effects mean I should contact your office immediately?
16. How shall I contact you if a worrisome side effect occurs? (Write down the phone number and who to ask for.) If you are not available, whom should I call?
17. What if my child skips a dose or spits it up?
18. Should I check in with your office before the next appointment to let you know how the medication is working? If so, when and how?
19. If I think of more questions later, how should I contact you?

Source: Linda Zweifel, Director of Programs, NAMI Montgomery County, Texas. Used with author's permission.

Look at the prescription before you leave the office, and ask the doctor to explain anything you don't understand. See page 34 for abbreviations often used on prescription forms and in records.

More About Meds

Psychiatric medications are drugs used for behavioral health problems such as mood or thought disorders (for example, depression and schizophrenia). Sometimes these are called psychotropic or psychoactive medications.

Most of the psychiatric medications prescribed for younger children are prescribed off label, which means the United States Food and Drug Administration has not yet approved these drugs to be used for that age group. So far the FDA has conducted very few tests of medications for children's behavioral disorders. Doctors use their own experience as well as the experience of other doctors and researchers to determine what drugs work best for children in each situation.

As with adults, medications don't work the same for different people. The doctor may have to try several drugs or combinations of drugs. It may take several tries to get the right dosage (amount of the drug). Sometimes the doctor will titrate a new medication (build up from a smaller to a larger dose over a period of days or weeks). This is done in order to find out what amount works best, or to cut down on possible side effects.

Some medications need to build up in the body over days or weeks in order to be effective. In a crisis situation, a doctor may prescribe an extra medication for a short time to keep symptoms under control until another medication has time to build up to a therapeutic dose (an amount that is effective for the child).

What to Know about Drug Warnings

New information about medications is always appearing. Sometimes a drug will be given a black box warning by the FDA, telling doctors to be careful about using the drug under certain conditions. (This term comes from the black outline put around these warnings in the Physician's Desk Reference or PDR, an important reference used by doctors to find drug information. The warning may actually appear in different forms elsewhere.) A black box warning doesn't necessarily mean the drug is dangerous under all conditions. Sometimes warnings are about not using certain drugs for certain disorders. Sometimes they warn about drug interactions, which means possible problems when one drug is used at the same time as another drug. Other warnings are for dangerous side effects that may (but don't always) occur and mean the doctor should stop prescribing that medication. If you see a black box warning on a drug your child takes, ask the doctor for more information.

It's important to learn about your child's medications. There are hundreds of drugs that can affect one another. Frankly, doctors are only human and may not always be aware of certain interactions or side effects. An extra pair of eyes on the task never hurts and often helps. You'll also know what to look for in side effects or danger signs so you can report them to the doctor right away.

PDR

The *Physician's Desk Reference* is available at many libraries. However, make sure the copy is no more than a year old, as medication information changes quickly.

Drug Samples, Titration, and Confusion

If your child is trying a new medication, the doctor may start you with free samples. He or she may say something like "Give her 10 milligrams for the first three days, then raise it to 20 milligrams for a week, then call and let me know how it's going." The trouble is that a sample package does not have your child's dosage on the label the way a regular prescription would. It's easy to get confused, especially when you are changing the dosage from day to day.

Ask the doctor to write down instructions for titrating medications. If you're getting a prescription, ask the doctor to write titration instructions on the prescription form. This will help to ensure that you get the right number of pills from the pharmacy. See Chapter 4, "Tracking Your Child's Progress," for an easy way to keep up with titration changes and record the results.

2 Getting Prepared
CONTINUED

Medication Abbreviations

Here are some abbreviations you might find on prescription forms, on orders for lab tests, and in your child's medical files:

b.i.d.	give twice a day
CBC	complete blood count
ECG	electrocardiogram (looks for heart problems)
EEG	electroencephalogram (looks for brain problems)
g	gram (unit of measurement)
h.s.	at bedtime
kg	kilogram
L	liter
mg	milligram
NSAID	Non-steroidal anti-inflammatory drug (such as aspirin)
O_2	oxygen
OTC	over-the-counter (non-prescription)
P.O.	by mouth
P.R.	rectally (in the child's bottom)
p.r.n.	as needed
q	every day
q.i.d.	four times a day
RBC	red blood-cell count
S.L.	sublingual (under the tongue)
t.i.d.	three times a day
WBC	white blood-cell count

Source: Linda Zweifel, Director of Programs, NAMI Montgomery County, Texas. Used with author's permission.

Chapter 3
Working with the Team

There Are No Stupid Questions

Remember to ask:

- Who?
- What?
- When?
- Where?
- Why?
- How?
- Can You Explain?

And write down the answers whenever possible!

Chapter 3: Working with the Team

As a parent, you are responsible for making sure the professionals on your child's team work together. That means you also have the right to be treated as a full partner. Even a good provider can get too busy, feel cranky, or jump to conclusions. If this happens all the time, you may need to find someone else. However, a good professional is more likely to treat you as an equal partner if you **show confidence in yourself.**

It doesn't matter that you don't have all the answers. Nobody does. However, each time you walk into a room to deal with a professional, remember: **As the parent of that child, YOU are in a position of authority, too.** Tennessee Voices for Children, a parent support and advocacy organization, offers these general tips on working with professionals:

1. **You have a right to be treated with courtesy and respect.** Everyone responds better if they are treated respectfully. You, the parent, know the most about your child. It's not acceptable for you to be treated as less than an equal.

2. **You know your child better than anyone else. Don't be intimidated by professionals.** They may know more about their profession, but you know your child best. You each have special knowledge that can help your child.

3. **Be as clear as possible.** Before an appointment, make notes to yourself about things you want to discuss with the professional. [See more about this on page 43].

4. **If you don't know how the professional came to a conclusion, ask for an explanation.**
A recommendation will always make more sense if you see clearly what led to it. Continue to ask questions until you understand the professional's thinking. **You may disagree with professionals about their recommendations for your child.** Don't be afraid to say so. Professionals aren't perfect. Sometimes they are mistaken. You know your child in a way they can't. If you think what they're suggesting won't work for your child, say so. Based on your input, professionals may change their recommendations.

5. **Explain your point of view in a calm, courteous way.** Don't attack the professional just because you don't agree. If you are calm rather than angry when expressing your opinion, the professional will be much more likely to see you as a partner who has a different point of view rather than as a "difficult parent."

3 Working with the Team
CONTINUED

Does the Plan Fit Your Child and Family?

Make sure the goals and objectives listed in your child's treatment plan fit the important concerns and symptoms you listed on the worksheets in this book. Do these goals make sense based on what YOU know about your child? Also, make sure the plan includes your role in treatment and the actions you will take. This might include some form of family therapy, changes in household routine, or new ways of dealing with your child's behavior. **Treatment should be aimed at healing the family, not just the child.**

It's okay to disagree, to express emotion, cry, or be angry, but if you are feeling out of control, it may be better to end early and schedule another meeting.

6. **If you need more time with the professional, say so.** If your appointment isn't long enough to get all your questions answered, the professional should be willing to schedule more time to meet with you. You are entitled to this. It may mean having to set another meeting on another day, but you have a right to get complete, clear information about your child.

7. **Keep in regular contact with any professional involved with your child.** In some instances, it's important to see a professional on a regular basis if you are going to get the best for your child. Check with professionals to see how often they recommend that you talk to them.

8. **Find a safe place to keep all of your child's important records.** Many parents find that the three-ring binder method described on page 21 works best. As time goes on, it will be essential to know what services your child received, from whom, and when.

9. **Encourage members of your child's team to talk with one another.** Part of your job as the coach of your child's team is to make sure the "team members" are all communicating. (See pages 38-41 for more tips on how to keep all the team members informed.)

10. **If you are pleased with a professional, say so.** Just like everyone else, professionals like to know when they are doing a good job. A simple "thank you" can mean a lot and will go a long way toward guaranteeing that they continue to do the best job they can.

11. **If you can't work things out with a professional directly, you may need to discuss your problems with a supervisor.** Make sure you've made every effort to resolve things with the professional before you see a supervisor.

12. **If you have tried all the above and still cannot get along with the professional, think about changing to a different person.** Sometimes people simply cannot get along. If you have done the best you can and still do not feel comfortable with the professional, you'll be better off finding someone else to help your family.

Adapted from: "Working with Professionals" by Tennessee Voices for Children. Used with permission.

How to Keep the Whole Team Informed

Picture your team standing in a circle. In the middle of that circle: you and your child. Say that one team member has an important piece of information they all should know. Let's call it the ball. Some parts of the team have a system for passing this "ball" back and forth. The process occurs most easily when they work for the same organization. However, doctors, therapists, and case managers may also need to communicate with insurance plans, social agencies, and schools. That's why you have to sign all those "permission to release information" forms.

However, many parents are surprised at how often they need to catch that ball and send it on to others. Here's an example of what can happen when a parent doesn't act to keep information flowing:

Let's say a child is showing new symptoms. The psychiatrist and parent agree to a medication change. However, nobody tells the primary care doctor. The psychiatrist doesn't know that the primary care doctor just gave medication for the child's winter ear infection. The two drugs may affect one another, but neither doctor is aware of it.

Meanwhile, the teacher notices the child is very sleepy in class. She hasn't been told this could be a side effect of the new medication. She thinks maybe his mother isn't getting him to bed on time. Nobody at the school calls his therapist or psychiatrist to say the child's grades are sliding downhill. The therapist may not know that school troubles are making the child feel more discouraged. Of course, neither the therapist nor psychiatrist has told the school about the new symptoms (which is why the child is taking those medications that make him sleepy). Though all the professionals in this example are doing the best they can, they aren't able to pass along all the information. The result is that nobody has all the facts they need to help that child.

The example above doesn't even include all those very common moments when the regular communication system breaks down. Sometimes important lab results don't show up before your child's next appointment. The referral phone call never gets made. A phone message gets mangled on its way between offices. Human errors will always happen, but a few tricks can help the information get where it needs to go.

One rule of thumb: If you can cut out a step that somebody else does, you can cut down the number of times it gets done wrong. Example: On some health forms and laboratory paperwork, you are asked to list doctors that should be informed of

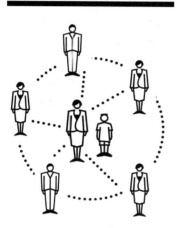

Passing the Ball

Professionals need the right information at the right time. Our health system and pure human error often put barriers in the way. It's up to you to keep the right information bouncing between members of your child's treatment team. The methods in this chapter can make passing that ball a lot easier

3 Working with the Team
CONTINUED

Forms, Forms, Forms

The Health Insurance Portability and Accountability Act (HIPAA) requires health professionals to get your consent when releasing information under certain conditions. In general, you will have to sign a release every time information is sent from one organization (such as your doctor's office) to another organization (such as the insurance plan administrators). **If you don't understand who will get this information and for what reason, don't sign until you get the answer.**

test results. **Make sure to have the names, addresses, and phone numbers of the doctors and others who should get copies.** (You can store these on the "Important Professional Contacts" form on page 41.) If office staff have to look up the address, the task may get put on the "hold" pile until someone has spare time.

Next, find out when the results will be ready. If the doctor needs them soon, call the office on that day to see if the results have been received. If the results have not shown up, your call will remind the staff to call the lab and ask about it. Before your child's next visit, check to see that test results have arrived.

Often there is only space for two or three names on that list of contacts, and sometimes the office will send results only to specialists involved in your child's care. (Remember, they may not be able to send your child's records to other providers without a signed release from you.) If you want schools, therapists, or others on the team to be informed, it may be easiest to send or bring copies yourself. You are the only one who always has permission to release information.

The 1-2-3 Method

When a report or lab test is expected, ask when you will get a copy. Always save this copy in your binder. Make additional copies and mail them with a cover note to other team members who need the information, asking each to include it in the child's file. **(If you don't want to write your own note, make copies of the "Keeping You Up to Date" form on page 40. You can also print it from the CD available for purchase at www.meltonhillmedia.com.)**

Here's the "1-2-3" method:

1. Bring a blank "Keeping You Up to Date" form to your child's appointment. Store a few cheap envelopes and some stamps in your binder.

2. Ask the doctor or therapist to fill in the basic facts about the change before you leave the office.

3. Drop this note in the envelope, address and stamp it, and on the way out, ask the staff to drop it in the outgoing mail.

NOTE: If making copies of reports and tests is difficult for you, ask the office staff if they can make an extra copy before you leave the appointment. Sometimes you can attach a note and they will slip it into an envelope and mail it for you. They may also be willing to fax the report. If you keep up a good relationship with office staff and don't burden them with too many requests, they are often willing to help.

Who Needs What

The need for a regular information exchange will vary according to who's on your team and what they need. Ask each team member, "Whom do you usually notify about a change in my child's treatment? Would you like to be notified when someone else makes a change? How would you like to get this information? Should I send it to you for my child's file? Should I just bring it the next regular appointment?"

Here are some general guidelines for keeping the professionals on your team informed of important changes:

For a MEDICATION CHANGE, tell:

- **Other doctors**
- **Therapists**
- **Case Manager**
- **School (This may include the teacher, counselor, or school nurse even if your child does not take these medications at school. Be sure to advise about possible side effects such as sleepiness or thirst so they can keep you informed. When they do, keep doctors informed.)**
- **Church or after-school youth group leader**
- **Parent who doesn't have custody, if child visits**
- **Childcare staff or other caregivers**

For a TREATMENT PLAN CHANGE, tell:

- **All doctors**
- **Other therapists**
- **School, if needed**
- **Others who observe the child's behavior (such as caregivers)**

For a MAJOR LIFE EVENT (such as a trauma), tell:

- **All major team members**
- **Others who care for your child**

"Keeping You Up to Date" Form

The form on the next page is a handy way to send along updates. Make copies and fill in the blanks. You may prefer to make up your own form or attach a personal note. It doesn't have to be formal. Just be sure it contains your child's full name, your name, and a contact phone number.

In notes to professionals, it's a good idea to include your child's date of birth and Social Security number because that's how many medical offices pull up your child's records from their computer systems.

Keeping You Up to Date

TO: _____

FROM: _____

DATE: _____

RE: _____
      (Child's name)

Date of Birth _____ Social Security Number _____

This note is to keep you informed of a change in treatment for my child. The following action has been taken by _____,
                                (Professional's name)

who provides _____
              (Treatment or service)

and may be reached at this phone number: _____.

☐ **Medication change:** From _____ To _____

☐ **Treatment Plan change:** _____

☐ **School IEP change:** _____
_____

☐ **Report, lab test result, or other paperwork (attached):** _____

Any other important change in my child's life:
_____
_____
_____

PLEASE INCLUDE THIS INFORMATION IN MY CHILD'S FILE.

If you need to discuss this change with me, I can be reached at:

_____. Times I can be reached at this number: _____.
(Phone number)

If you don't have a release form on file for the professional named above, please contact me.

Thank you for helping to keep my child's health information up to date!

Important Professional Contacts

This page can help you keep track of contact information for your team. Put in the professional's full name and role on the team (for example: Dr. Susan Smith, psychiatrist). You may want to gather business cards from each professional you visit with your child. Put these cards in your binder's zipper pouch, and fill in this chart as you get time.

Team member: _____
Role on the team: _____
Organization: _____
Address: _____
_____
Phone: _____
FAX: _____
Office hours: _____

Team member: _____
Role on the team: _____
Organization: _____
Address: _____
_____
Phone: _____
FAX: _____
Office hours: _____

Team member: _____
Role on the team: _____
Organization: _____
Address: _____
_____
Phone: _____
FAX: _____
Office hours: _____

Team member: _____
Role on the team: _____
Organization: _____
Address: _____
_____
Phone: _____
FAX: _____
Office hours: _____

Team member: _____
Role on the team: _____
Organization: _____
Address: _____
_____
Phone: _____
FAX: _____
Office hours: _____

Team member: _____
Role on the team: _____
Organization: _____
Address: _____
_____
Phone: _____
FAX: _____
Office hours: _____

Team member: _____
Role on the team: _____
Organization: _____
Address: _____
_____
Phone: _____
FAX: _____
Office hours: _____

Team member: _____
Role on the team: _____
Organization: _____
Address: _____
_____
Phone: _____
FAX: _____
Office hours: _____

3 Working with the Team
CONTINUED

Meds Safety

See Chapter 4, "Tracking Your Child's Progress," for more tips on organizing medications, observing side effects, and keeping track of behavior changes.

Get to Know Your Pharmacist

A good pharmacist could be your single best source of information about medications. Most are willing to spend time making sure you have all the facts. Pharmacists also know a lot about your prescription drug insurance.

Try not to use more than one pharmacy. If that's not possible, use the same chain. The stores in one chain will usually have the same computer system to hold patient information. (Often you may need to tell them where to look for it.) It is VERY important that the pharmacist know all the medications your child is taking, including over-the-counter drugs. It is also very important that the pharmacist have all information about any other medical needs.

Always check the label on the medicine bottle to make sure the details match the prescription form. Pharmacists may substitute the less expensive "generic" for a brand-name drug. That's fine so long as the doctor has not marked "name brand only" on the prescription. Also, look at the drug information inside the prescription envelope, medicine box, or flyer. Ask about anything you don't understand. Check for stickers on the bottle that give warnings such as "take with food" or "avoid sun exposure" and ask for more details. (What kind of food? Can I give this an hour after my child eats? My child plays on a team outdoors. If I put a strong sunscreen on him, is that good enough? What does "drink plenty of water" really mean? How much should she drink? How often?)

Ask about side effects, even if the doctor has already mentioned this. A busy doctor may not tell you everything (or know everything) about a medication. Ask which side effects mean you should check back with the pharmacy or doctor right away. If you notice a side effect that wasn't listed, follow up with a phone call. Often a pharmacist will do further research to find out what's happening. Unlike doctors, pharmacists can usually answer questions on nights and weekends and will get right on the phone with you. Often, they can also call the doctor's office directly and get faster answers.

Be sure your child's pharmacy record includes any over-the-counter (non-prescription) drugs your child takes. Ask about meds for temporary illnesses such as colds, infections, or viruses. If for some reason the pharmacist is not helpful with answering questions, think about using a different pharmacy.

Take time to form a good relationship with your pharmacist. Plan ahead to get refills. Use automated refill phone lines and automatic refill reminder systems if they are offered. Ask what times of the day or week the store is busiest. Try not to call with questions or prescription needs during "rush" hours, so the pharmacist can give you the attention you need.

Amazing but True

The busy doctor who seems to rush you out the door all the time will almost always stop and listen IF you bring along a written list of questions. **The key is a written list.** *For some reason, this tactic is not as effective if the questions aren't written down on an actual piece of paper or in a notebook. The paper itself seems to provide a visual cue to pay attention!*

Refer to the list when speaking, for example saying, "Let's see— I have just two more questions here." This is a well-tested method for getting a professional to slow down and provide the information you need. Also, doctors and clinicians respect a parent who seems organized— and who expects a full response.

Making the Most Of Appointment Time

1. **Be on time for the appointment.** If you have to cancel, give 24 hours notice whenever possible. Some offices charge for appointments that are cancelled without notice, and insurance companies don't pay for that charge. Take along the office number. If you are stuck in traffic and have a cell phone, call and tell them the reason. Most offices will give you a 15-minute "grace period." If you are later than this, they may ask you to reschedule.

2. **Before each appointment, make a written list of what you need to tell or ask the doctor.** Be brief and stick to the point. Take out your list and refer to it as you speak. Put the most important matters first.

3. **Know your own listening style.** Some people find that jotting down what the other person says helps them focus better. However, if writing things down will distract you, consider bringing along someone else to make notes.

4. **Repeat what the professional says in your own words.** (This is known as "mirroring" or making a "Reflective Response.") You might say:
   - In other words…
   - So what you're saying is …
   - As I understand it, you mean…
   - Am I correct that you want…
   - Let me make sure I've got this right…
   - Then you would agree that…

   This gives the team member a chance to correct or add to the explanation. Don't be embarrassed if you heard imperfectly. Your team member wants you to understand.

5. **Before you leave, check that the doctor has given you all necessary prescriptions, medicine samples, instructions, and paperwork,** and make sure you have placed these things in a safe spot. Many things are forgotten in the last rush of a short appointment.

3 Working with the Team
CONTINUED

You Have to Be Creative

One mother of a child with severe ADHD would sometimes call ahead to see how late the doctor was running that day. If he was 30 minutes behind schedule, the receptionist gave the mother permission to arrive a bit later.

The father of a child with autism would wait in the car with his son, letting him play with a favorite toy. The receptionist would call the father's cell phone when the doctor was ready, so they were able to walk right in.

Waiting Room Survival Tactics

For families with younger children, a 30-minute wait in the outer office can seem endless. Plan to bring some favorite books or small toys to keep youngsters occupied. Check out the room on a first appointment so you can get prepared for next time. Is there somewhere your child can have a healthy snack while waiting? Is it possible for your child to play a little outside before going in? Is there a convenient restroom to visit before you enter?

If waiting is a big problem, discuss this with the professional. Finding ways for your child to improve "waiting" behavior can sometimes become part of the treatment plan.

One parent who worked long hours made a deal with her six-year-old that waiting-room minutes would be their "special time" to read, color, play a game, or talk together. The child started to look forward to these times, and waiting-room behavior improved.

Rehearsing the proper waiting-room behavior with your child can make a difference. ("In the waiting room, we keep an inside voice. You need to sit quietly in a chair and look at your book. When the nurse calls us, you'll put the toys away. Then we'll walk into the doctor's office, and you'll go sit in the brown chair.") Rehearse the same behavior every time you visit the office. Possibly offer a small reward or privilege for following your rules. Again, try to get paperwork done ahead of time so you won't need to fill it out while keeping an eye on your child.

These days, many office waiting rooms that serve children include a VCR or DVD player to show movies. That can be great unless your child wants to keep watching when your turn is called! If so, try rehearsing this transition with your child: "When the nurse calls your name, I'll count to five and you'll start walking towards that door. If you're inside before I say "five," you will earn… If you aren't in there, you will NOT earn…." Sometimes the staff will be willing to turn off the player until your child leaves the waiting room. (They don't want to deal with a meltdown any more than you do!)

Bear in mind that a waiting room is not a good place for a "showdown" with your child. Yelling at, swatting, or spanking your child will not do much good. Also, it definitely will not give the professionals in that office a positive view of your parenting skills. Try to stay cool. Be honest with the professional and staff about difficulties with controlling your child's behavior. Mention what works in other situations. They see this kind of thing all the time, and your conversation may spark some good ideas. Remember, this is just one more problem to be solved by cooperation between you and your team.

Advocacy Groups Can Help

Family advocacy organizations can help with advice or letter-writing. In some cases, a member of an organization will go with you to a meeting or appointment.

What to Do When Someone's Not Listening

Problems happen. People don't always get along. You may be denied services or feel your views are not being heard. Whatever the situation, it's up to you to act like a "parent professional." Here are some suggestions from Tennessee Mental Health Consumers' Association:

Approaches that are likely to work:

- Allow mental health providers to be human. They will do what they can; you do what you can.
- Learn what services you can expect from your providers.
- Learn about agency grievance procedures. (Note: These are steps you have to take when making a formal complaint about a professional or about the services you receive.)
- Learn about the services and resources available in your community.
- If you have a complaint, keep a written record of what happened. Include dates, names of those involved, witnesses, and specific details.
- Go to the person who can make the decision you are asking for. If a problem cannot be resolved on one level, take it to the next.
- Be polite, but keep asking until you are satisfied.

Tips for Success:

- If you have a problem with a provider, first talk to him or her about it before going to someone higher up in the agency.
- Listen to the provider all the way through, just as you like to be heard.
- Politely insist that the provider listen to you all the way through. Give details to back up your points.
- If the problem is resolved, thank the provider.
- If you are not satisfied, take your concern to the next level. Keep going up the chain of command until you are satisfied.
- If you are still not satisfied, file a written grievance (letter) with the agency, government mental health authority or behavioral health organization. You have a right to a copy of the results of each grievance.
- Contact an advocacy organization to help you.

*Reprinted from **BRIDGES: A Peer-Taught Curriculum on Recovery from Mental Illness** by Sita Diehl, MSSW, Barbara A Nelson, and Elizabeth Baxter, MD. Reprinted with permission from NAMI Tennessee and Tennessee Mental Health Consumers' Association.*

3 Working with the Team
CONTINUED

Learn More

How to Get Services by Being ASSERTIVE, *by the Family Resource Center on Disabilities, is a manual for becoming more effective in the way you deal with professionals, organizations, and the people in your life. Send $12 to Family Resource Center on Disabilities, 20 E. Jackson Blvd. #300, Chicago, IL 60604.*

Practicing Assertiveness

The way you speak, move, dress, and react can affect how you are treated by professionals. Assertiveness experts offer these tips on getting results at an appointment or meeting:

Project the right image.

- Dress neatly. "Business casual" clothes are better than jeans or shorts.
- Greet people firmly. Make strong eye contact.
- Take time to organize records and paperwork.
- Sit or stand in an upright but relaxed way. Keep your body still and relaxed. Fidgeting makes people seem uneasy or lacking in confidence.
- If you feel nervous, practice what you want to say ahead of time.

Speak with confidence.

- State clearly and calmly what you believe to be true ("I think that... I feel that...").
- Speak up in a strong tone of voice without asking for permission or making apologies.
- Don't try to attack, bully, blame, or shame the other person. Your goal is to solve problems, not win arguments.
- Listen to the other person carefully. Show you are listening by wearing an alert, attentive expression.
- Refer to the other person's point of view when you give a different opinion ("I understand that you feel...but I believe...").
- When you honestly agree with the person, say so. A little stroking never hurts ("Yes, that seems like a good idea.").
- Don't raise your voice. If you aren't satisfied, say so politely but firmly. Make suggestions. Ask for ideas.

Show you expect results.

- Before you leave the room, briefly sum up the discussion, describing what each person has agreed to do.
- State decisions in terms of "we" and "us" ("So, as I understand it, we've decided to..."). Remember, you are the other vote in the room.
- If you think the other person may not clearly understand or stick to the agreement, send a note that sums up the decisions made in your meeting. Keep a copy for your files. In case of a conflict, this letter becomes part of the record to help you get results.

Sources: ***How to Get Services by Being Assertive*** *by Family Resource Center on Disabilities and* ***Assertiveness Step by Step*** *by Windy Dryden.*

Chapter 4
Tracking Your Child's Progress

Be Good to Yourself

Sometimes parents of children with behavioral health problems can get very overwhelmed. A different system can help. Talking to other parents in the same situation can help. The important thing to remember is that you are not a failure because things aren't working out. See Chapter 7, "Coping with Crisis and Healing the Family," for more on how to cope.

How to Be a Good Observer

As a parent, you serve as the eyes and ears of the treatment team. For a "medication management" visit, your child may spend as little as 15 minutes once every few weeks with a psychiatrist or nurse. A therapy session will usually be less than an hour once or twice a week. These professionals have a lot of knowledge about **why** children behave the way they do and **how** certain behaviors can change. You are the one who can tell **what** your child is doing most of the time. You are the best one to gather this information from other caregivers, such as your child's teacher, other relatives, youth-group leader, or childcare staff. Your job as the team's parent professional is to:

- Give medications in a safe, organized way.
- Observe how the treatment affects your child's behavior in everyday life.
- Watch for any danger signs and take prompt action to get help.
- Report facts clearly to the treatment team.

For a busy parent with a difficult child, this can seem impossible. What if you make a mistake with medication? How do you know what side effects to look for? Who has time to write down all the details of a child's behavior when every day is a new struggle? What if you just aren't a very organized person?

The good news: You don't have to be neat, organized, or any kind of expert to do the tasks listed above. The best tips and tools for doing this job come from parents who don't have time and patience for a lot of paperwork.

The most important tool is a regular parent check-in routine that FITS YOUR PERSONAL STYLE. Everybody functions better when a few things are done the same way every day. We are more likely to stick with routines that are so simple we don't even need to remind ourselves to do them after a while. You probably have some of these routines in your life already. Maybe you do certain things when you get up in the morning, right after a meal, or just before bed.

The key is to link this parent "check-in" routine with other natural routines in your life. That way, when the unexpected happens, you are more likely to go back to these tasks. For example, let's say that after your kids are in bed, you take time to relax for a little while and have a snack. Then you get things ready for the next day. So you decide that after you relax for a bit and before you start preparing for the next day, you'll pull out the binder (or go to the computer) and make a few notes about your child.

➡

4 Tracking Your Child's Progress
CONTINUED

Pill Refill Routine

Refill the pill organizer on the same day each week. This is a good time to check the front of the bottle for the number of refills left. Check the dosage, too. Use the Medication Log on page 51 to cut down on mistakes.

Maybe you decide to spend 10 minutes updating some of the worksheets in this chapter. If you do it every school night, that's all the time it takes. If you miss a few nights because something else happened, you go back to this habit when you can return to the regular routine.

Keep this routine simple and short. Give yourself time to get used to it and don't feel guilty if it doesn't always work. Many parents like to attach the check-in routine to something pleasant, like having that snack, drinking a cup of coffee, or sitting in front of the TV set. Also, it's a good idea to make sure materials such as your binder and a pencil or pen are stored in the same convenient place so you don't have to use that check-in time to hunt for what you need.

Avoiding Medication Mixups

A good routine is the key to giving medications safely. If your child takes regular doses of more than one drug, keep these medications sorted in a seven-day pill organizer. Buy this small, inexpensive plastic box at any pharmacy. The organizer makes it much easier to give meds accurately on a busy school morning when everybody is rushing out the door. You can send the box along when the child goes to stay with other relatives or caregivers. Also, you can see at a glance if a dose has been missed. Put vitamins and other over-the-counter medicines your child takes in the same box.

Medication Safety Tips

- GIVE THE EXACT DOSE. If the medication comes in liquid form, use a special measuring tool such as a medication cup or spoon, a dropper, or a syringe. Sometimes the tool comes with the medication. Ask the pharmacist about the best tool to use. If you have to split pills, you may want to buy an inexpensive pill-cutter from the pharmacy.

- STORE MEDICATIONS AT THE RIGHT TEMPERATURE. Many drugs are sensitive to heat and may become less effective. Some parents keep a small container with extra meds in a purse or car. If so, make sure the meds are securely stowed and don't get overheated.

- STORE MEDICATIONS IN A SAFE PLACE. If young children are in the house, use childproof caps.

Lock 'Em Up

The safest way to store medications is in a locked box or cabinet. You can buy this kind of box at most discount or hardware stores. Some health and social agencies require parents to keep medications locked up.

- NEVER give more or less of a medication than the doctor prescribes. NEVER stop giving a medication without talking to the doctor.

- ASK THE DOCTOR OR PHARMACIST what to do if a dose is missed or spit up. Follow these instructions carefully.

- KNOW WHAT TO DO IN CASE OF AN ACCIDENTAL OVERDOSE. If the child doesn't show immediate symptoms of illness, call your pharmacy or local Poison Control number (in your phonebook). In a crisis situation, call 911 for help, and ask to be connected to Poison Control for more advice until that help arrives.

- LET OLDER CHILDREN SHARE RESPONSIBILITY FOR MEDICATIONS. It's a good idea for older teens that are medically stable to begin learning how to take and keep track of their own medications. They will need this skill as young adults. However, just like learning to drive or manage money, this is a transition that has to be carefully supervised by parents. Talk to your child's doctor and therapist about how and when to start this process. Encourage your child to use the check-off worksheets in this chapter.

- PREVENT TEEN PRESCRIPTION DRUG ABUSE. Teens should not have access to medicines they don't take. Keep these out of sight and reach. Many young people will experiment by helping themselves to prescription drugs in the house. This is a growing problem that can lead to injury and death. Talk to your child about this issue. Watch out for peers that may look for prescription drugs in your house or influence your child to do so.

- MOST OF ALL, if your child is severely depressed or at risk of self-injury, lock up all medications. An overdose of the drugs could be used on impulse with tragic results. If you don't know whether this is a concern, talk to your doctor.

4 Tracking Your Child's Progress
CONTINUED

Read More on Meds

Straight Talk About Psychiatric Medications for Kids by Timothy Willens, MD (The Guilford Press, New York, 2004. Third edition, September 2008.) *helps parents understand what the major medications are and how they work. Important technical terms used by doctors are defined in easy-to-follow boxes scattered throughout the book. Tables and medication logs are printed in the back. This is a good source for browsing.*

Keeping a Titration Record

If a medicine is being **titrated** (gradually increased over days or weeks), you will need to keep the dose straight and observe results. An easy method is to use the inexpensive calendar you put in the front of your binder (see page 21). In each day block, write the medication name and correct dose for that day (example: 5 mg at breakfast, 5 mg before bed).

Put a check by that medication name when the dose is taken. At the end of the day or the next day, you can jot down a few words about side effects and results (example: "Less appetite. Got all homework done without prompting").

This gives you a simple and accurate day-to-day record of how the medicine worked at different levels. At the next appointment, you can show this calendar page to the doctor. It will help him or her determine the right dose for your child.

Other Easy Tools For Tracking Progress

When your child settles in to regular dosages of medications, you'll still need to keep a record of changes over time. Your child's reactions to the medications may change over time for many different reasons. On the next three pages are logs you can use to:

- **List regular medications**
- **Record side effects**
- **Make simple notes about special behavior episodes that you want to discuss with your team.**

You can bring the doctor, nurse or therapist up to date by showing these charts at each appointment. Keep all the charts for a year in your binder. Without much effort on your part, the team will have a detailed home record of your child's progress over time.

Your Child's Medication Log

This chart helps keep information on medicines in one place. Keep an updated version in your binder to bring to appointments and use when talking to doctors by phone. Put a copy inside the medicine cabinet or lockbox to use when you refill weekly pill containers. (Tip: If you fill in this sheet by hand, write the "last updated" date in pencil. You will need to change it each time you add to this list.)

Make sure the school, each of your child's doctors, and all caregivers have an updated version of this list.

Child's name: _____ Pharmacy name, phone number: _____

Last updated: _____ _____

Name of Medication/ Date Started	Total Dosage (Example: 40 mg)	Directions: How Much/When/Special Instructions (Example: 20 mg tablet morning, 20 mg tablet evening/Take with food/Avoid sun)	Refill Number	Doctor/NP's Name/Phone Number

Over-the-counter (non-prescription) medicines, vitamins, and herbs (including amounts and when taken):

Special notes for teachers and caregivers (other instructions, side effects to watch for, what to do if side effects are observed):

Medications Side Effects Checklist

Make one checklist for each medication your child takes. (Ask older children to complete this.) Take it along to the next appointment. If any terms on this sheet are unfamiliar, ask your pharmacist or doctor to explain.

Child's name: _____ From Month/Day _____ to _____

Medicine: _____ Dose: _____

SYMPTOM	YES	NO	OTHER COMMENTS
General Body Functions			
Mouth feels too dry			
Drooling or too much saliva			
Lost weight			
Gained weight			
Constipation			
Nausea			
Vomiting			
Trouble urinating			
Urinating frequently			
Blurry vision			
Problems with sexual function			
Change in breasts			
Changes in menstrual periods			
Headache			
Lightheadedness, dizziness			
Sleep			
Sleepiness, sleeping a lot			
Trouble getting to sleep or staying asleep			
Muscles and movement			
Feeling restless or jittery, cannot stay still			
Muscles stiff			
Slowness, trouble getting moving			
Shaking or muscle trembling			
Mental function and attitude			
Memory problems, forgetful			
Low energy, easily tired			
Difficult to concentrate			
Too much activity or "pressured" speech			
Irritable			
Anxious			
Thoughts about self-harm			
Any other symptoms			

Adapted with permission from Linda Zweifel, Director of Programs, NAMI Montgomery County, Texas.

Your Child's Behavior Log

Behavior Log for: _____

Medications: _____

Log begun (month, day, and year): _____

Date	What happened or what was the behavior?	Where and when did the behavior take place? (Example: At school, during recess, while doing homework.)	What was taking place right before the behavior happened? (Example: Change in family plans, child told "no" about something he wanted, argument with sibling.)	Other comments, details, or factors involved? (Meds change? Illness? Event in family?)	What happened after the behavior? (Action you, others, or the child took.)

Chapter 5
The Classroom-Treatment Connection

Ten Ways to Be a Great Advocate for Your Child in the School System

1. **Be willing** to get involved.
2. **Be prepared** for school meetings.
3. **Be careful** to get the facts before you sign anything.
4. **Be firm** with the team about setting practical goals that help your child make real progress.
5. **Be flexible** about how to reach those goals.
6. **Be available** when the school needs your help.
7. **Be alert** for problems with the plan.
8. **Be open** to creative solutions.
9. **Be ready** to keep learning.
10. **Be good to yourself.**

What Your Child Needs to Succeed

Keeping up with schoolwork is one of the toughest challenges faced by a child with behavioral health problems. For example, difficulty with controlling anger, following rules, or working in a group can be enormous barriers to achieving in school. Certain disorders can hinder a child's ability to see a task through from beginning to end or to switch from one task to another. Sometimes, a child feels too hopeless or anxious to make an effort. If medications are needed, it might take a while to get the dosages right—and meanwhile, the child may be too sleepy, hungry, or jittery to concentrate. When the child has more than one problem, it's tough to know exactly what's happening and why.

Federal education law gives special rights to students with disabilities, including those caused by behavioral health and developmental disorders. The trouble is that laws tend to come with complicated rules, forests of paperwork, and plenty of room for disagreements. Sooner or later, most parents of a child with behavioral health problems will feel confused, frustrated, upset, or angry about school services. Some parents think schools simply don't want to provide the assistance that their child needs. Some schools think that parents ask for too much, help too little, and expect too many miracles. Sometimes both sides can be right. To create an educational program for a child with special needs, the parents and school have to cooperate with and respect one another.

By learning to be an effective parent advocate, you can fight less and get more help for your child. An advocate speaks on behalf of someone else who needs support. An advocate gathers facts, helps to plan a strategy for reaching goals, and works with others to find solutions. Your job as a parent advocate is to:

- **Learn what your child needs to make progress at school.**
- **Work with the school team to plan practical goals and the right educational program to meet those goals.**
- **Make sure that this plan gets put into action—and help to change it if necessary.**
- **Form a good relationship with school staff so that everyone on the team can work for your child's success.**

You don't have to be an expert, and you don't have to do it alone. As with so many things in life, just "showing up"—being there and being aware—is half the job. Along the way, you may need to ask others, such as a family advocacy organization or a professional on your child's team, to provide information or speak up for your child's interests. However, the parent is always a child's most important advocate. You know your child better than others do. Also, the school system needs your permission to change your child's educational program, unless you can't or won't get involved.

Beware of Too Much Information

Books, articles, classes, brochures, and websites offer huge quantities of advice about how to get school services for children with disabilities. (In fact, a recent Internet search on the words "special education" produced **812 million entries**!) With so much material out there, it's easy to get discouraged about what you don't know. You may feel guilty that you don't have time to read everything or don't understand a lot of what you read. You may worry that people will talk you into doing the wrong thing. You may feel intimidated by school officials who use unfamiliar terms—or act as if they have already decided what your child needs. On some days, you may think: *I don't really know what to do, and nobody will listen to what I say, anyway. So what's the point of trying?*

The cure for information overload is to take a deep breath, relax, and start from wherever you are. Prepare for one meeting at a time. Remember: It is the school system's legal responsibility to help you understand the process. So one important way to learn is to ask lots of questions before, during, and after school meetings.

The School's Special Role on Your Child's Team

Each member of your child's treatment team has a different job with a different set of rules. Federal education laws define the rules for teachers and school officials on your team. Because of these laws, health professionals and school professionals must look at your child's symptoms from two different points of view. Health professionals treat physical, behavioral, and developmental symptoms in order to help a child function better in all parts of everyday life. But under the law, a school system can only provide special education services for symptoms that are the major cause of a child's learning problems and can't be handled in a regular education program.

The Basic IDEA

The **Individuals with Disabilities Education Improvement Act of 2004** (often known as **IDEA 2004**) is a federal law that guarantees the right to educational services for students aged 3 through 21 who have disabilities. All states must follow this law. Under IDEA 2004, your child has a basic right to **free appropriate public education (FAPE)** that is "designed to meet his or her unique needs." When the regular education program cannot meet those needs because of a disability, your child has a right to certain **special education services** provided by the school system at no cost to you. **Special education** is the overall term for the methods and services that schools use to educate students with disabilities.

No Time? Build a Read-It-Later File

Too busy right now for classes or long books about special education? Start a file of free materials and "read 'em when you need 'em." Schools and community mental health organizations often give out short, simple fact sheets or brochures produced by family advocacy groups and professional organizations.

Stick these papers in a file folder, or punch three holes in a large mailing envelope and put it in the back of your binder. With this method, you can pull out something for a quick read as you sit in a doctor's waiting room or get ready for a school meeting.

The important thing is to start learning. It will make you feel more comfortable with the process, and you'll have a better idea where to go for more information when you need it.

5 | The Classroom-Treatment Connection
CONTINUED

Ready to Learn More?

Each state has at least one Parent Center. A Parent Center offers free training sessions that teach parents how to get the right school services for children with disabilities. You can also call or write for help with questions or problems that have to do with school special education services.

For information, check out the Technical Assistance Alliance for Parent Centers, www.taalliance.org or call toll-free 888-248-0882.

A Diagnosis is Not Enough

Your child does not get services under IDEA 2004 just because he or she has been diagnosed with a behavioral health disorder. Before the school system provides any special services, it must go through a series of steps to prove that your child's problem has **educational impact** (sometimes called **impact on educational performance**). This means the problem is the main reason your child is not learning as much as others the same age can.

In order to decide whether your child's disorder has educational impact, the school is required to gather **evidence**. A parent or teacher may feel strongly that a child needs help—but this is not evidence. Evidence is a set of facts that can be observed or measured. If you understand what kinds of evidence the law requires and how that evidence is gathered, you can help your child get the right services.

Below is a short description of how a child is **certified (made eligible) for special education services.** The chart on page 62 also shows the basic steps a school and the child's parent must take. You have a legal right to be involved in every part of this process. It is very important to play your part to make sure your child gets the services he or she needs.

STEP 1 | The school receives a request to evaluate your child.

Let's say your child gets distracted easily and has problems sitting still to do regular activities. You take the child to a psychologist who says the child has ADHD (Attention Deficit Hyperactivity Disorder). This is called a **clinical diagnosis**. But having this diagnosis is not enough to make your child eligible for special education services. A **school evaluation** must show that this problem meets certain **criteria** (standards) under IDEA 2004 rules. This evaluation is also called a **comprehensive assessment** because it usually examines many areas of the child's behavior, abilities, and performance at school. Even if a child has been diagnosed by a health professional, the school system must do its own evaluation.

A parent, teacher, other school staff member, or state child protection agency has to ask for this evaluation IN WRITING. When the school system gets this letter, it must either start the process for getting an evaluation, or turn down the request. If your request is denied, you can **appeal** (ask a higher authority to decide this issue) by using procedures called **due process rights**. If you don't understand the written explanation the school provides, school staff must try to explain it to you.

Don't Wait Until Kindergarten!

Well-meaning friends, relatives, or other people around you– including your child's doctor– may say things such as "Don't worry, the child will grow out of it." Don't wait! If your instinct tells you something is wrong with your child, ask for an Early Intervention Services or Child Find evaluation.

To get details about the EPSDT program in your area, call your local health department.

Before the school can start an evaluation, you must sign a permission form. The form explains what areas of the child's functioning will be examined and why. The form may list the name and phone number of a school staff member to call for more information about the evaluation. (If not, contact the principal.) You can ask what tests will be used, what they measure, and what you will have to do. You can give this person information from other professionals on the team, or you can ask that they be contacted. You will probably be asked to sign release forms that allow the school to get information from other sources. (Look back at page 28 for good questions to ask about an evaluation.)

If your child has not yet started school

IDEA 2004 gives parents the right to ask the Department of Education for a free evaluation of their child under 3 years old to determine if he or she is eligible for early intervention services. These are services to help very young children with medical, behavioral, or developmental problems. If your child is eligible, a service coordinator will be assigned to your family to work out an Individualized Family Service Plan for getting your child the help he or she needs. Your child's doctor can arrange for an evaluation if he or she feels your child has a problem.

Children aged 3 through 5 can be evaluated through the Child Find program provided by every school system. School staff will examine whether your child is likely to develop problems or delays in learning. If the child qualifies, he or she can get free special education services from the school system, such as a free preschool program. Call the local school system office or school board to find out how to request an evaluation. Also, you can look for Child Find under school system listings in the phone book. If public health insurance covers your child, the Early, Periodic Screening, Diagnosis, and Treatment program (EPSDT) can assist you. **These evaluations are free.** Getting these services early in life can be very important to your child's future.

STEP 2 The school system gathers information about your child.

The school system forms an assessment team to evaluate your child. For a behavioral health issue, the assessment team usually includes a school psychologist. It may also include specialists in speech and language, occupational and physical therapy, academic subjects, or certain disorders, such as autism. The team gathers information using the following:

- Standardized tests, checklists, and a health history.
- Observation of the child doing ordinary activities such as working

5 The Classroom-Treatment Connection

CONTINUED

Special Education Disability Categories

A child must be certified to receive special education services under one of these 13 categories defined by IDEA 2004:

- *Autism*
- *Deaf-blindness*
- *Deafness*
- *Emotional disturbance*
- *Hearing impairment*
- *Mental retardation*
- *Multiple disabilities*
- *Orthopedic impairment*
- *Other health impairment (ADD/ADHD)*
- *Specific learning disability*
- *Speech or language impairment*
- *Traumatic brain injury*
- *Visual impairment*

A good source of information about what these categories mean is **A Parent's Guide to Special Education** *(AMACOM Press, New York, 2005). In this book, school psychologists Linda Wilmshurst and Alan Brue also include a good summary of what to expect from a school evaluation.*

---

in class or playing on the playground. Sometimes this observation may include a home visit.

- Information reported by parents, teachers, and others involved in the child's treatment or daily life.
- Evidence of methods the school has tried to deal with this problem in your child's regular education program, and how these efforts worked. (This is called Response to Intervention.)

 STEP 3 **The evaluation must show evidence that your child's problem has educational impact.**

The school psychologist and others who are evaluating your child have to make written reports about test results, observations, and other information. They look to see if three eligibility criteria (standards for qualifying) have been met:

- **Your child is making less than expected progress in school.** Expected progress means how much state and federal standards say a child of that age should be learning during the school year. In a preschool child, it means there is evidence that the child is not developing some learning skills at the expected rate and is "at risk" for making too little progress when he or she enters school.

- **Your child's problem is the MAIN REASON that he or she is making less than expected progress.** If other factors —such as lack of certain academic skills, or lack of ability to speak English—are the main causes, a behavioral health issue alone won't qualify your child. These other causes are called rule-outs.

- **Your child's problem falls within one of the 13 disability categories listed under the IDEA 2004 law.** Some behavioral problems diagnosed by health professionals (such as conduct disorder or oppositional-defiant disorder) are not included under this law, even if they interfere with learning. The evaluation must show that your child's condition fits into one of the categories listed at left.

If all three criteria are met, the child is considered to have a disability (also called a disabling condition) and has the right to get services under IDEA 2004. The assessment team will offer the evidence and make recommendations. However, the actual decision about whether your child is eligible for services is made at a meeting between YOU and staff from the school system. If you DON'T get involved, the school system staff can meet and make these decisions without you. If you DO get involved, the school system must meet with you and get your permission for the next steps. **GO TO THIS MEETING IF YOU CAN!**

What's a "504 Plan"?

Section 504 of the Rehabilitation Act is a civil rights law that guarantees access to education for children with disabilities. 504 Plan *accommodations are changes that assist children with special needs in a regular education program. Some children that don't qualify for special education services under IDEA 2004 will qualify to receive accommodations under Section 504. To get these accommodations, a school evaluation must show that the condition interferes with the child's ability to learn. The accommodations are described in a 504 Plan document signed by the parent and the school system representative.*

STEP 4 **An IEP meeting is held to decide whether your child is eligible for special education services.**

The parent and a school system representative meet with members of the assessment team and other school staff. This is called an Individualized Education Program (IEP) eligibility meeting.

NOTE: "IEP" is an abbreviation that schools tend to use three different ways. It can be used to mean the meeting itself, the education plan written at the meeting, or the legal document produced in this meeting. The people involved in this meeting—including you as an equal partner with the school—make up the IEP team.

The eligibility decision has two parts. First, the team decides to certify your child in one of the 13 types of disabilities listed under IDEA 2004. Educational law does not use the same categories that health professionals do. For example, a child with ADHD is certified under the category "Other health impairment." Mood disorders such as depression are classified as "Emotional disturbance." If a child also has another difficulty, such as a hearing problem, "Multiple disabilities" might be chosen. As a parent, you can give your point of view or present evidence about which category is best.

If you agree with the school system's decision to certify your child in the disability category chosen, you sign the first part of the eligibility report. The school system's representative also signs.

Next, the team must decide whether reasonable changes in the regular education program will be enough to help your child make the expected progress. If these changes (called accommodations and modifications) are enough, the child won't qualify for special education services. However, he or she may get these changes through a 504 Plan (see "What's a 504 Plan?" at left). To learn more about how this decision is made, see "The Story of Jenny and John" on page 61.

If you and the school system representative agree that the regular program cannot meet your child's needs, you both sign the second part of the report. At this point, your child is now eligible for special education services. However, there are still many decisions to be made (and forms to fill out) to create the IEP document. The next part of the process is to decide exactly what kind of special education program your child will receive.

STEP 5 **The IEP team writes an education program to meet your child's special needs.**

This step may occur at the same meeting as the certification decision in Step 4, or it may be saved for a later meeting if the team needs more time. The IEP team writes a plan to help your child make educational progress. By law, all plans must have three basic parts:

5 The Classroom-Treatment Connection
CONTINUED

Who's on the IEP Team?

Many school professionals may be needed for your child's IEP meeting. Most often, they include:

- *Principal;*
- *School psychologist;*
- *Classroom teacher (often, this is the homeroom teacher if your child is in middle or high school);*
- *Any specialists that have tested your child or have special knowledge about the issues;*
- *Special education teacher;*
- *Supervisor, in some cases;*
- *Someone from a special classroom or school if the school system is proposing such a placement for your child;*
- *You, and*
- *The child, beginning at age 16, or younger when necessary.*

- **Goals** for how much progress your child can be expected to make this year, what the steps toward making this progress will be, and how the progress will be measured.

- **Placement** in a regular or specialized classroom based on what is needed to achieve the goals. Some children receive special services in the regular classroom or outside the classroom for part of the day. Others may be placed in special classrooms at the regular school or in special schools with other children who have similar disabilities. In some cases, a teacher comes to teach a child at home for a short period. Sometimes, a child with problems the school can't handle must be placed in a residential school or hospital.

- **Related services and supports** that will help the child make progress toward the IEP goals. These services might include speech therapy, psychological counseling, or special equipment.

The decisions made by the IEP team are written into a standard set of forms. As soon as you and the school system sign it, this IEP document becomes a legal contract that describes what the school system promises to do in order to meet your child's special needs. Signing this form means you give permission for those actions. To make sure you understand what you are signing, the school system is required to explain all parts of this IEP document to you. The school system must also provide a foreign-language or deaf interpreter if you request that service.

You do not have to sign this document if you do not agree with all of the decisions proposed by the school system. If you disagree, you and the school will need to meet again to work out your differences. If you still can't agree, the IDEA 2004 law and state procedures offer ways to appeal. If the school system does not carry out the plan as promised, you can also appeal. However, you and the school system must make every effort to agree on a plan. You must try to communicate with each other if problems come up as the plan is used.

Showing written evidence that you have made a **good-faith effort** (tried to be fair, sincere, and involved) is important in case you ever need to file an appeal to get your child services. This effort will also help to create a good relationship with the school so the plan will work better. (See more about written evidence in "Tips for Writing Letters.")

STEP 6 The school system meets with you once a year to review the IEP.

A new IEP must be completed and signed one year from the date the old one was signed. This **annual review** of the IEP often begins in the spring so the school can start your child's new program in the fall. However, if the IEP was signed at a different time of year, the new IEP must be completed a year from that date.

At this meeting, the goals and objectives are reviewed to see what progress your child has made. Goals may be added in, taken out, or changed in some way. Based on the new set of goals, the IEP team considers whether your child's placement or services need to be changed. The IEP team always includes YOU.

An IEP can be changed more than once a year. If your child's condition changes or the plan isn't working well, either you or the school can request a meeting to revise the IEP at any time. Sometimes the parent and school can agree (in writing) to small changes without holding a meeting. However, you can always ask for a meeting if you feel one is needed. The school evaluation that started this process must be updated once every three years. You don't need to make another request for this evaluation, and the school doesn't need your permission.

Sometimes a separate plan is written to provide a summer program called an Extended School Year Program (ESY) so that your child can keep up the progress he or she has made.

The Story of Jenny and John

Here is an example of two cases in which the same clinical diagnosis might lead to kids' getting different services in school.

Imagine two children named Jenny and John. Each one has been diagnosed with major depression. At this point, medications and therapy work well for Jenny. The former "A" student has become a "B-minus" student this year, but her annual test scores show that she is making enough progress in a regular education program to keep up with state standards.

To help her progress, Jenny needs some modifications in the usual classroom routine. For example, she needs to be able to leave the classroom for a mid-morning snack because the medications she is taking make her very hungry and less able to concentrate. The teacher has also created a quiet place in one corner of the room where Jenny can go if she's having a bad day. Unless something changes for the worse, Jenny's depression may not be considered a disabling condition that makes her eligible for a special education certification. However, the modifications in her regular education program are written into a 504 Plan document signed by her parents and the school system.

John, on the other hand, is falling behind. He missed a lot of school days last year because medications and therapy have not been able to control his depression. Test scores show he has not made enough progress to keep up with other students his age. The teacher reports he can't work on projects with other students. The school evaluation has ruled out other causes for this lack of progress. John's depression appears to have educational impact. If the regular education program can't be modified to meet his needs, the IEP team may recommend that John be certified to receive special education services.

You Don't Have to Go It Alone

Many parents feel uncomfortable facing a room filled with school staff members. If you are one of those parents, plan to bring someone with you. It doesn't have to be an expert. You can bring a relative or friend who takes notes or observes what goes on at the meeting.

You are also entitled to bring:

- *Your child's other parent, even if he or she does not have custody;*
- *Other professionals on the treatment team, or outside experts who know about the issues;*
- *Someone from an advocacy organization to give you advice and support.*

If you plan to bring others, let the school know, ahead of time, who will attend.

How Your Child Gets Special Education Services

The Basics:

- A federal law called the Individuals with Disabilities Education Improvement Act (IDEA 2004) guarantees that a student with disabilities will receive a "free appropriate public education" that is "designed to meet his or her unique needs."
- When the evidence shows that your child's educational needs cannot be met in the regular program because of a disability, he or she has a right to special education services.
- **TO GET THESE SERVICES, THE PARENT AND SCHOOL MUST GO THROUGH THE STEPS BELOW.**

STEP 1

The school receives a request to evaluate your child.

Your child has symptoms:
- physical
- behavioral
- developmental

If your child gets a clinical diagnosis from a health professional....

....**Your child still needs a *school evaluation* to be certified to receive special education services.** A request for a school evaluation is made in writing by:
- you (the parent) OR
- your child's teacher OR
- other school staff OR
- a state child protection agency

If the school DOESN'T AGREE, you may appeal this decision to a state agency, using **due process rights.** The school must explain these rights.

If the school AGREES, you must sign a form giving permission to evaluate your child. The **Parent Consent form** includes:
- areas to be tested
- why these areas are being tested.

STEP 2

The school system gathers information about your child's condition, abilities, and school performance.

A school **assessment team** is formed to evaluate your child. The team usually includes the school psychologist and may include other school specialists, depending on the child's problems.

The team gathers information using:

- Standardized tests, checklists, and health history
- Observation of the child
- Information reported by you, the teachers, and others involved in your child's education or treatment
- Evidence about methods the school used to handle the problem in the regular program (**Response to Intervention**).

62

STEP 3

The evaluation looks for evidence that your child's symptoms have educational impact.

The assessment team makes a written report that includes:
- Test results
- Information it gathered or observed
- Recommendations about whether your child is eligible for services.

For your child to be eligible, the evidence must show that his or her disability meets three *eligibility criteria* (standards):
- Your child is making less progress in school than the state expects for a child the same age (or your child is "at risk" of not making this progress, if preschool age).
- The disability is the **main reason** your child is not making the expected progress. The evidence must **rule out** other causes, such as lack of ability to speak English.
- Your child's problem fits the criteria for one of the 13 disability categories under federal law.

STEP 4

The IEP Team meets to decide whether your child is eligible for special education services.

The decision to *certify* your child for services is made at an *Individualized Education Program (IEP)* meeting.

The people at the meeting make up the *IEP team*.
- The IEP team includes a school system representative, other school staff, or experts in certain disabilities.
- **YOU are on the IEP team, as an equal partner with the school.**
- The meeting may also include someone you invite to offer information or support.
- The school principal, classroom teacher, or homeroom teacher will usually be present.
- Members of the assessment team report test results, observations, and recommendations.

If the evidence shows your child meets the criteria, he or she will be *certified* (declared eligible) in one of 13 *federal disability categories*. The disability categories are not the same as those used in a clinical diagnosis.

| If you and the school system representative AGREE to have your child certified under a certain category, you both sign the IEP eligibility form. | If you DON'T AGREE, you don't sign. You and the school system try to work out differences. | If you CAN'T AGREE, you can appeal to a state agency, using your due process rights. |

STEP 4 CONTINUED

If reasonable changes in the regular program can help your child make enough progress, your child will not be eligible for special education under the IDEA 2004 law.

However, your child may get certain services in the regular classroom under Section 504 of the federal Rehabilitation Act. This is called a **504 Plan**.

STEP 5

The IEP Team writes an educational program to meet your child's special needs.

This step may occur at the meeting to certify your child or at a later meeting.

The IEP team makes decisions about:
- **Goals** for the kinds of progress your child should make in different areas of educational need by the end of the year. This includes the specific steps for making this progress, as well as how and when the progress will be measured;
- **Placement** in a regular or special classroom, special school, or other setting;
- **Related services and supports** that can help your child reach the goals.

The decisions made by the IEP team are written into a set of forms called the **IEP document**.

| If you and the school system representative AGREE to the decisions, you both sign this set of forms. | If you DON'T AGREE, you don't sign the forms. You and the school system try to work out differences. | If you CAN'T AGREE, you can appeal to a state agency using due process rights. |

When you and the school system reach an agreement, the forms are signed and the child can begin receiving special education services on the date written in the IEP document.

STEP 6

The school system meets with you at least once a year to review the IEP.

A new IEP must be written every year. This is called an *annual review*.
- The IEP team reviews how the goals were met.
- Goals may be taken out, added, or changed.
- Based on the new set of goals, the team will review whether your child needs any changes in placement or services.
- At every IEP meeting, you have the right to show new evidence, state your concerns, suggest ideas, and ask questions.

An IEP can be changed more than once a year if conditions change or if the plan isn't working well. Either the parent or school may request a meeting to *modify* (change) the IEP.

The school evaluation must be updated at least every three years.

THE BOTTOM LINE ON THE IEP:

BE THERE and BE AWARE

You have a right to attend the IEP meeting. Be there if you possibly can.
▶ The school must tell you the time and date of the meeting at least ten days in advance.
▶ If you can't come, let the school know right away and suggest other dates. The school must try to find a date and time when you can be there. Sometimes you can even meet by phone.
▶ If you can't be there, the school needs to keep you informed of the results by phone or mail.

You have a right to have all parts of the IEP explained to you.
▶ The school system is required to use a set of printed forms. The forms have many pages and technical terms. The staff must explain all the details in words you can understand.
▶ Don't sign anything if you don't understand or don't agree.
▶ Don't be embarrassed to keep asking if something doesn't make sense. You may see a flaw that nobody else has noticed.
▶ Don't feel rushed because the meeting is taking a long time or people in the meeting need to leave. The school system must keep meeting with you until the whole job is done.

An IEP meeting is just the beginning.
▶ After the meeting, a parent needs to stay involved. Set up a regular way to communicate with your child's teacher.
▶ If your child is having a really tough time, or if parts of the plan do not seem to be working, meet with the teacher and other school staff to brainstorm ideas.
▶ Even if you don't have much time, let the school know you are willing to help solve problems with your child's program.

5 The Classroom-Treatment Connection

CONTINUED

Go to the Source

The source most often quoted in books and websites about special education is **Wrightslaw**, *the website and book series produced by attorney Pete Wright and psychotherapist Pam Wright. Browse through* www.wrighslaw.com *for almost anything you need to know about your child's educational rights. You will also find detailed advice about working effectively with the school system.*

The Wrights' handbook, **"From Emotions to Advocacy: The Special Education Survival Guide"** *(Harbor House Law Press, Inc., Hartfield, VA, 2007) is well-organized and easy to skim as you get ready for the IEP meeting. Also included are sample letters and helpful worksheets for keeping records.*

What to Do Before the Meeting

Getting prepared for an IEP meeting is very important, but it doesn't have to be difficult or stressful. Below are the main areas to consider:

✔ **Get a date that works for you.** At least 10 days in advance, the school system must send a notice with the date, the time, and the place where the meeting will be held. There may be a name and phone number on the form (if not, call the principal to get the name and number of a person you can contact about the meeting). If you can't be there, call the person named on the form right away to reschedule a new date and time. The school must try to plan the meeting at a date and time you can attend.

You don't have to wait for the school to set the date. "When you know your child's annual review is coming up, pick up the phone and suggest days and times that are convenient for your family, as well as other persons and professionals you might be inviting to attend the IEP meeting," says education attorney Gary Mayerson in his book **How to Compromise With Your School District Without Compromising Your Child** (DRL Books, Inc., New York, 2004).

Better still, send an e-mail or drop off a note at school. When it comes to IEP meetings, it is always better to "do it in writing and get it in writing." (See more on "Tips for Writing Letters," page 76).

✔ **Find out what the meeting will cover and how long it will last.** The purpose of the meeting should be listed on the notice. If you aren't sure, call and ask what this includes. Mayerson also suggests that once the meeting date is set, you should find out how much time is scheduled for the meeting: "If the response is '30 minutes' and you have half a dozen problems to discuss, you know that the allotted time frame will not be sufficient. You should ask for more time or a different day for the IEP."

✔ **Let the school know who you will bring, what you need, and what you want to discuss.** A parent advocate's rule of thumb: *Surprises are not a good thing at an IEP meeting.* Just as the school should tell you what to expect, you should tell the school what you want. This shows courtesy and good faith. It also lets others prepare, which means less wasted time at the meeting. Your consideration encourages the school to show you the same courtesy and respect.

Let the school know as soon as possible who will come to the meeting so they can plan to have enough space. If you feel it is necessary to tape-record the meeting, notify the school because school officials will want to do the same. Ask for any special services you need, such as an interpreter. You may write this request in your own language; the school is required to get it translated.

Prepare Yourself

Look back at "Practicing Assertiveness" on page 46 for tips on looking and acting like a "parent professional." If you are nervous about speaking up in a meeting, write down a list of points you want to make, and practice saying them in a strong, direct way. Ask a family member or friend to listen to your points and look over your list of concerns.

The more familiar you are with special education terms, the more confident you will feel. Flip through your information file or go to some of the special education websites listed in this chapter.

If you are in touch with others through an advocacy organization or support group, call your contact person for a last-minute boost of confidence.

☑ **Look at your child's school records.** The law gives you the right to see your child's permanent record (usually known as a cumulative record or CR) if you make a request in writing. You are granted this right by IDEA 2004 and the Family Education Rights and Privacy Act (FERPA). You should ask to look at the entire CR as well as any other school system files that have information about your child. However, the school has the right to charge you to make copies of these files, and the CR of a child with problems tends to have a lot of pages. Many parents prefer to go to the school or school system office, look through the file, and copy only the material they need for the issues at hand. (Others feel it is necessary to have a copy of everything. Do what seems right to you–it is always possible to change your tactics later.)

In either case, make sure you get copies of these important documents:
- Any past tests or evaluations you don't already have.
- Any past IEP forms you don't have.
- Letters sent between you and the school, if you don't have copies.
- Any letters, reports, or notes by school staff about your child's behavior or performance.

☑ **Prepare your list of concerns and questions.** For a shortcut, look back at the "My Child's Strengths and Needs" list on page 7. Which of these apply to your child's behavior and performance in school (or attitude toward school)? Put those at the top of your list of concerns. Look through your child's file and list any questions that occur to you. Add any questions about the evaluation process or test results you have already reviewed. NOW, go back and try to narrow down the list to five or six items. Think about wording. Focus on the result, not the service. Rather than listing an item as "Getting Tommy a classroom aide," you may want to list "How can we make sure that Tommy finishes assignments without needing the teacher's constant attention?"

☑ **Prepare your "Meeting Toolkit."** Plan to bring your binder to the meeting, because you may want to refer to documents. Some parents like to put sticky notes on the edges of the reports or documents they are most likely to need. If you need to pull out a document to show it to others at the meeting–or if someone needs to copy something–make sure to get your original document back. ***Don't forget to take your list of concerns.***

☑ **Other items to bring:**

Notepad or notebook paper. Some parents like to take notes on paper inside the binder. Others like to use an inexpensive, three-hole-punched notebook that can be removed for the meeting and placed back in the "School" section of the binder afterwards.

5 The Classroom-Treatment Connection
CONTINUED

Take Care of Your Documents

NEVER write on original documents except very lightly in pencil. Don't use a marker or highlighter pen. You may need to copy those documents to send to others when making a request or appeal. NEVER send your original documents to anyone. Keep them in your binder or files. If someone at an IEP meeting wants to copy one of your original documents, DO NOT LEAVE IT BEHIND. Get it back in your binder before you walk out the door.

Writing materials. At least two pens, a pencil, highlighter, and sticky notes.

A picture of your child. Many IEP meetings include experts or school officials who have never met your child. Passing around a picture helps the meeting focus on a child, not a "case." One father used a series of pictures taken at different seasons to show how his child's mood went up in the spring and down in the winter.

Any documents you have sent the school or the school has sent you that relate to this meeting. You may need to show that you made certain requests or sent information on a certain date. Having a dated document to pull out will prevent lost time and arguments. If these documents are filed in your binder, mark them with sticky notes on the edges so you can find them when needed.

Other support materials. Bring any outside evaluations or letters about your child's disability, even if you have already given copies to the school. If possible, bring one extra set in case the school staff needs it.

Food and drink. IEP meetings can sometimes go on for hours, and you will not be at your best when you are hungry and thirsty. As a friendly gesture, some parents like to bring snack foods or a bowl of candies to share. At least make sure that you have water or your favorite beverage to keep you going.

What to Expect During the Meeting

The agenda. The IEP meeting may have a written agenda that is passed out to everyone at the table. If you don't get one, politely ask the facilitator (that is, the person who runs the meeting) to list the main points that will be covered. Write them down. You will need to look at them as the meeting goes on. A typical IEP meeting usually begins in this way:

Statement of purpose: At the start, a facilitator will usually state the purpose of the meeting, saying for example, "We're here today to determine Mary's eligibility for services." If this is not the purpose stated in the notice you received, ask why.

Introductions: Next, everyone present should be introduced by name and job title. Again, if this doesn't happen at the start of the meeting, ask for it. (See "Tricks for Remembering Who's Who" on page 71.)

Parent's concerns: The next item of business in a good IEP meeting is to ask the parent to list concerns about the child. These concerns are placed in the formal IEP document. If this item does not appear at the top of the agenda, politely suggest that you would like to mention these concerns before any test results or recommendations are discussed. Say something like, "I want to be sure everyone is aware of these concerns so they can keep them in mind when they explain each part of the evaluation to me." Take out your list and read it to the group. It isn't necessary to discuss your concerns at this point unless someone else has a question. However, keep the list handy. Before the meeting ends, you will want to check that everything has been covered and that all your questions have been answered.

Present Level of Performance. This means the results of your child's evaluation and other comments from the people in the room. This information will be summarized in the IEP document and used to build your child's educational program.

How to Listen to Test Scores

It can be very painful to sit there, trying to look calm and collected, while other people give you bad news about your child. However, it is really important to understand this information. The evidence contained in all those strange-sounding words will be used to establish your child's eligibility for services. It will also be used to determine what types of services your child will receive. Here's what often happens—and what you can do to get a grip.

The scene: A crowded IEP meeting full of school staff. When the meeting started, you were introduced to five new people. You have already forgotten at least three names.

The action: A school psychologist pulls out several sheets of paper covered with numbers and graphs. Words such as "percentile rank" and "processing speed" begin to fill the air.

Your inner response: TMI (Too Much Information)! CUT (Can't Understand This)! Help!!

Your outer response: "Oh...umm...yes...I see... right."

Instead, you could say:

- "Sorry, this seems very confusing. Could you run that by me again...?"
- "I'm not really a math person. Are you saying...?"
- "What does this mean in terms of my child's ability to...?"
- "Can you explain why...?"
- "Do you think these results are a true reflection of my child's performance in...?"
- "So, if you had to sum up this set of results in one sentence..."

TAKE YOUR TIME. Don't feel rushed because others in the room seem impatient or start having side conversations. Test scores confuse many parents. School specialists are not always good at explaining complicated matters in simple terms. You can help them practice this important skill! Most school personnel want you to understand what test scores mean so you can understand their recommendations.

Get a Head Start

If possible, meet with the school psychologist, reading specialist, or other evaluators ahead of time to review test results. You will feel less pressured, and it will give you a chance to get better prepared for the IEP meeting. If you forget to ask about something (or the information fades out of your brain by the next day), write down those questions to bring to the IEP meeting.

Let the school know well in advance that you want to meet with an evaluator to review test scores. Some parents include this request when giving permission for the evaluation by attaching a note or writing the request directly on the bottom of the form. As with anything you sign, KEEP A COPY.

5 The Classroom-Treatment Connection
CONTINUED

Get the Final Draft

The results of an evaluation may be in "draft" (unfinished) form at this meeting or at the IEP meeting. In some cases, that happens because the evaluator wants you to look over the report for anything that is incorrect or has been left out.

Ask the psychologist or other school specialist when a final copy will be ready. Request that it be mailed to you or left at the school for you to pick up. When it comes, file this report in your binder under the "School" section. If it doesn't arrive, ask again. If you see any errors in this copy, write a note to the principal asking to have the errors corrected and a new copy sent to you. Keep all the versions, but (lightly, in pencil) mark the last one "Final" at the top of the first page.

This report is important *because it becomes part of your child's permanent record and is used to create your child's educational program.*

See the IEP in 3-D

Many parents think IEP teams meet to discuss and "vote" on a child's program. Not true: An IEP team tries to reach **consensus** (general agreement) on issues but does not actually make the final decision. The various teachers and experts are present to offer information, write goals, make recommendations, and brainstorm ideas. All final decisions are made by **two equal votes**. The parent gets one vote. The other goes to the system representative, also known as the **Local Education Agency (LEA) representative**. This person is assigned to represent the school system during the meeting.

The system representative's signature on the IEP forms will legally **obligate** (require) the system to take the actions described on those forms. Your signature as a parent means you give **consent** (legal permission) for the school to take those actions. When—and only when—the two of you sign, it's a deal. Everyone else signs the forms to show they attended the meeting, as well as checking a box to show their agreement or disagreement with the decisions made.

Why is this important? Because an effective parent advocate sees a meeting in "3-D Vision." A 3-D approach means you **D**eal **D**irectly with the **D**ecision Maker. Here's how to do it: Listen carefully (with an alert, interested expression) to every person's comments. HOWEVER, when you want to make an important point or request (as in, "I feel that..." or "Would it be possible to...?"), talk directly to the one person in that room who has the most power to say "yes" to what you want. In an IEP meeting, the **system representative** has the power to agree or disagree with your requests.

The system representative is often, but not always, the highest-ranking person in the room. This may be the school principal or the special education supervisor. If you are not sure, politely ask before the meeting begins, "Who will be serving as the system representative today?" Before the meeting starts, make sure your seat at the table allows a clear view of this person. If not, say, "Could we shift around? I want to be sure I can see everyone. That spot would be best for me, I think."

Sometimes the system representative will have to duck in and out of the meeting to take phone calls or deal with problems elsewhere. If that happens, try to restate important questions or requests again when that person returns ("Mrs. Blank, while you were out, I mentioned that...What is your feeling about this?"). If that doesn't seem possible, make a note to bring up your point when the goals are being written ("Mrs. Blank, earlier when you were out, I mentioned...and I believe we never resolved...").

Why 3-D Vision works: When you give the decision maker your attention, you don't waste time trying to talk others into changing their opinions. You put the decision maker in the position of speaking for the whole group. That person is more likely to listen directly to what you say and to tell you clearly what the school system is willing to do.

Tricks for Remembering Who's Who

The IEP team will often include several people whom you have never met. Some of these people may be school specialists who evaluated your child. Others may be experts brought in to give advice or school officials from higher up in the chain of command. Introductions are usually made at the start of the meeting, but it's hard to absorb this information when so much is happening. You may feel embarrassed to ask people's names again.

There are three good reasons to keep a firm grasp on knowing who's who: First, it is more courteous and professional to address people by name. Second, you need to know which person is the speech pathologist, which one is the resource teacher, and so on, so that you can understand the information each person is presenting. Third, you may need to contact some of these people later.

At the beginning of the meeting, try one of these methods for connecting names and faces.

Business card "bingo": Ask each member of the team to give you his or her business card. Ask anyone who doesn't have a card to write the name and job title on a small piece of paper. Lay these cards out in front of you in the same pattern that people are seated at the table. Glance down at the cards when you need to jog your memory.

Seating chart: Draw the table's shape on a piece of notebook paper. Outside the "table," make a circle for each person at the meeting. Pass the paper around, starting at one corner of the room, and ask each member of the team to print his or her name and job title in or near the circle that goes with that position at the table. Then put this paper in front of you so you can glance at it when you need to.

Ask someone at the table to help you organize the cards or start the seating chart. **Getting others involved can actually be a great icebreaker, because almost everybody has trouble remembering names.** Also, it will help save time and let you give full attention to the meeting.

Put a star next to the person who is acting as system representative as a reminder to keep your focus on him or her. After the meeting, write the date on this paper and file it with your meeting notes in the "School" section. Keep all business cards!

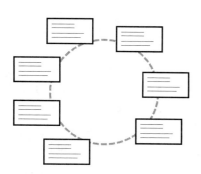

Business Card Bingo

Lay business cards out in front of you in the same pattern that people are seated at the table.

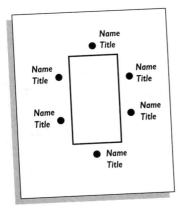

Seating Chart

Ask each member of the team to print his or her name and job title in or near the circle that goes with their position at the table.

5 The Classroom-Treatment Connection

CONTINUED

Great Guide

The Complete IEP Guide: How to Advocate for Your Special Needs Child (NOLO, Berkeley, California, 2007) by attorney Lawrence M. Siegel provides a detailed blueprint for developing your child's educational plan. Laws are explained in plain language. Tear-out forms in the back of this book offer terrific fill-in-the-blank letters, information logs, and worksheets, such as an "IEP Material Organizer" sheet and a checklist for when you visit your child's class.

Building Goals That Really Work

Some parents walk into an IEP meeting thinking, "My child needs..." a certain type of classroom or service (such as speech therapy, a personal aide, or a particular teaching method). Sometimes those parents are right about the service—but wrong about how the IEP process arrives at those decisions. This can cause a lot of conflict.

In the IEP process, all decisions about your child's program begin with GOALS. These goals are written into the IEP document, along with a series of details about how your child should make progress toward the goals. Based on what is needed to meet those goals, your child is placed in a certain kind of classroom and receives certain types of services.

Just as a house needs to be built on a strong foundation, the IEP needs to be built on strong goals. Weak goals are general statements of what a child should know or become. There is no clear way to show if the goal has been reached. Strong goals identify specific, practical skills and specific methods for producing evidence that your child has learned that skill.

Many parents feel totally lost when the team starts writing IEP goals. The IEP forms contain many codes, percentages, abbreviations and tiny check-off boxes with terms such as "Criteria for Mastery." Don't panic. You aren't picking up a hammer and nails to build this house by yourself. You are working with the builder (your school system) to make sure this house has all the right parts. If you know what the main parts are, you can ask the right questions.

How Goals Are Built

Your child's evaluation (together with other input at the IEP meeting) is summarized on a part of the IEP document called **present level of performance**. It identifies your child's **areas of need**, which means the broad categories of skills in which your child needs to make progress. Areas of need might relate to academic areas (for example, "Math Reasoning") or how a child gets along with others and deals with emotions (a "Social/Emotional" area).

For each area of need, the IEP team writes an **annual goal** that sums up the overall progress it is hoped your child will make in the coming year. Underneath this annual goal will be a description of the specific skills the child will learn, along with how and when those skills will be measured. These details are usually called **objectives** or **data points** because they describe ways that school staff will be able to tell whether your child has learned that skill.

The Four Building Blocks of a Strong Goal

Let's say a child named James has an area of need called "Written Expression." This category includes skills such as handwriting, spelling, and learning to organize ideas. At the top of the goal sheet, the IEP team writes a broad annual goal they want James to reach by the end of the year. This might be, "James will achieve functional writing skills at the fifth-grade level."

One of the objectives under this goal is to improve James's spelling skills. To build a strong overall goal, this objective should contain four strong building blocks called **CONDITION, BEHAVIOR, ACCURACY, and RELIABILITY**.

Let's say that one of the objectives under James's goal is to improve his spelling. Here's how the building blocks will show up:

- **CONDITION:** This means **how** or **when** James will do something to show he has learned the skill.
  Example: "When prompted by staff no more than three times to get his materials ready and begin work, James will…."

- **BEHAVIOR:** This means **what** the child is expected to do.
  Example: "…complete a fifth-grade level spelling test…."

- **ACCURACY:** This means **how well** the child must do this task.
  Example: "…with 80 percent accuracy…." (this means James spells 8 out of 10 words on the test right).

- **RELIABILITY:** This means **how often** the child must do this behavior accurately in order to show "mastery" (prove the goal has been met).
  Example: "…in three out of five trials." (This means, for example, that on a weekly spelling test, James will get an 80 percent score on a spelling test at least three weeks out of every five weeks he takes a test.)

Strong goals have three important qualities. A strong goal is **CONCRETE**. It describes exactly what sorts of tasks the child has to do in order to learn that skill. "James will work cooperatively and independently with others" is not as strong as "James will work in a small team of at least two other students to complete a project without direct support from staff."

A strong goal is **MEASURABLE**. It tells how information will be gathered about whether the goal was reached. "Teacher observation" is not as strong as "With staff help, James will be able to describe at least four ways he contributed to the team's work."

A strong goal is **TIME-LIMITED**. That means the staff knows when and how often the task must be measured. For example: "By the end of the first nine-week grading period, James will complete at least two team projects with other students."

Parent Advocate's Motto

One mother pasted this note to the inside front cover of her binder so she would be sure to see it at every school meeting: "I DON'T know everything—but I DO know how to ask questions about everything."

Do Your Child's IEP Goals Pass the Building Blocks Test?

This worksheet can help you do a quick "building inspection" on your child's goals. It can be used at least four ways:

1. **USE IT FOR EACH GOAL.** During an IEP meeting, ask a school staff member to help you fit the parts of the goal under each building block. You can use one blank sheet for every goal. Some building blocks may be written on the IEP form using codes and numbers. Ask the team to explain it in simple words. If one building block is not filled in–or you don't understand the words used–this goal may need more work. NOTE: This exercise can encourage team members to slow down and explain technical terms.

2. **USE IT AS A WARM-UP.** You can use this sheet during an IEP meeting for the first one or two goals as a way to help the team "learn" how to explain it to you. This reminds everyone that you will insist on strong goals that include these building blocks. The discussion will tend to shift in that direction.

3. **USE IT AS A REFERENCE.** You can keep this sheet in front of you as a reminder of the building blocks--and as a way to make notes about questions to ask.

4. **USE IT AS AN EXERCISE.** You can do this exercise on your own, using the goals on your child's old IEP or another child's IEP. The more you practice, the easier it is to spot the strengths and weaknesses of an IEP goal.

Area of Need (Example: Written Expression): _____

Annual Goal (Example: "James will gain functional writing skills at the fifth-grade level"):
_____

CONDITION: This means how or when the child will do something. (Example: "When prompted by staff no more than three times to get his materials ready and begin work, James will….")
_____
_____

BEHAVIOR: This means what the child is expected to do. (Example: "…complete a fifth-grade level spelling test….") _____

ACCURACY: This means how well the child is expected to do it. (Example: "…spelled with 80 percent accuracy," means eight out of ten words will be spelled right.) _____
_____

RELIABILITY: This means how often the child must do it accurately to meet the goal. (Example: "…in three out of five trials," means James will spell enough words right at least three times for every five tests.)
_____
_____

FINAL INSPECTION Is this goal:

☐ **Concrete?** Does it describe exactly what sorts of tasks the child has to do in order to learn that skill?

☐ **Measurable?** Does it tell how information will be gathered about whether the goal was reached?

☐ **Time-limited?** Do the staff members know when and how often the task must be measured?

Follow-Up is Important

Although an IEP form is long and complicated, many small details of the plan may not be written down. By writing a short thank-you note to the school system representative, you put those details on record and make sure busy staff remember to do as they promised. For example, the letter might say:

Dear Mrs. Blank,

Thank you for a productive meeting to create my daughter Anna Carter's IEP. It is my understanding that the school psychologist, Dr. Ken Brown, will call me within two weeks to review Anna's reading test scores, which were not available when we met yesterday. Meanwhile, Mrs. Maria Smith has agreed to be my contact person for questions, and will get back to me within a week to schedule another IEP meeting.

If this is not your understanding, please contact me at the phone number listed above. I look forward to working with you again.

Sincerely,

Jean Lopez

Before You Leave the Meeting

☑ **Review all decisions.** The person in the room who is recording decisions should read everything back to the team. Listen *very carefully*, and interrupt politely if anything is incorrect or has been left out. Feel free to do this as many times as necessary. If something went by too fast to sink in, ask the person to read it again or show it to you.

☑ **Sum up** any matters that are not written into the IEP or have been left for next time. ("OK, my understanding is that we've decided to…, and our next steps will be…") Make sure it is clear WHAT will happen, WHO is responsible for those next steps, and WHEN they will happen. It's a good idea to request that these details be written into the meeting notes, which become part of the IEP document. Ask whom you should contact if you have any further questions about the IEP document later on.

- **Remember to take copies of all documents you signed.**
- **Remember to take all the documents and materials you brought with you to the meeting.**
- **Remember to thank everyone for taking part in your child's meeting.**

What to Do After the Meeting

☑ Give yourself credit for doing your job as a parent advocate. Many parents forget this important step. You deserve a pat on the back for trying to find your way through a difficult process.

☑ File all documents back in your binder as soon as possible. Go back to your notes and fill in any details while your memory is still fresh. If someone took notes for you, fill in any extra things you remember.

☑ Put any important meeting dates or deadlines on the calendar in the front of your binder. For example, if the school psychologist promised to send you a corrected copy of the psycho-educational evaluation report in a week, mark that date on your calendar as a reminder to call if you don't get it. If the IEP team needs to meet again to finish working on goals, pencil in a reminder to check back in a week if you haven't received notice of a meeting date.

☑ Reread the IEP document carefully. Make sure you understand the contents, and if not, call the "contact" staff person with questions.

☑ Send a short thank-you note to the system representative. If the school principal did not fill this role at the meeting, send him or her a copy of the letter.

5 The Classroom-Treatment Connection

CONTINUED

Reminders for Letter-Writers

A letter is a record of what happened. It must be written so that someone who was not part of the events (like a special education supervisor or hearing judge) can understand clearly what happened. When you write a letter:

1. *Use your child's name in the letter.*
2. *Use your full name.*
3. *Add who you are if your last name is different from your child's. For example: Mary Green (mother).*
4. *Date the letter.*
5. *Include your address and phone number.*
6. *Sign the letter.*

NOTE: Always keep copies of all e-mails and letters you send to the school system. Put these in your binder.

Tips for Writing Letters

Attorney Pete Wright, co-author of many educational advocacy books and the website www.wrightslaw.com, says, "If it was not written down, it was not said. If it was not written down, it did not happen." He means that you need to be able to prove by written evidence that things happened the way you say they did.

Many people don't like to write letters or feel they don't know how to do it well. However, a letter can very simple and still do the job. Great letters can be a big help, but "good enough" letters are better than phone calls or casual talk. It's okay to use a form letter such as the samples you find in many guides and special education websites. It is usually better to type a letter, but a neatly handwritten note can be fine for sending everyday information, like a message to a teacher.

Here are a few important reasons for writing letters rather than simply talking to school staff, social services agencies, etc.:

1. A statement in writing is a permanent record.
2. You can think out exactly what you want to say and double-check for errors.
3. If you are upset, you can wait to "cool off" before you reply to another person's words or requests.
4. A letter makes it less likely that people will misunderstand, ignore, or forget what you want.
5. In a letter, you can state (for the record) a reasonable time for getting a response to your request. (Example: "I look forward to getting your response within ten days.")
6. In many cases, the law requires the school system to respond or take action within a certain time after getting your letter. This is called a timeline. Your letter or signature on a form may begin a timeline for getting your rights or your child's rights.

For better results, a letter should be addressed to a specific person. Call the school or agency to ask for the right name (and be sure to spell it correctly!). Add the person's title or office for the record. (Example: Mary Jones, Principal, Happy Valley Primary School.)

Sources: Support and Training for Exceptional Parents, STEP Record Keeping Information Packet, www.wrightslaw.com, Tennessee Voices for Children (www.tnvoices.org).

Start Early, Dream Often

*Although a child who gets special education services must have a transition plan in place by age 16, the process can start sooner if the school system and parent agree that doing so is **appropriate** (necessary and practical) in order to help a child learn certain skills by the time he or she leaves high school.*

Whether or not a formal transition plan is written, it's a good idea to begin thinking about life after high school as soon as the child enters his or her teen years. Some independence skills may take a long time to learn. If you know the long-term goal, your child's annual IEP goals can begin to include some of these skills.

At your child's annual review, ask the principal to make sure the subject of "planning for transition" gets put on the agenda. It may spark ideas for tomorrow that affect today's educational program.

Transition Planning With Your Teen

Transition is a term used in education law to mean a period of years between the late teens and early twenties, when a young person's task is to gain the skills needed for independent living. This passage is never smooth or easy, but it can be especially tough for kids with behavioral health problems. A child who has spent years struggling to cope with difficult symptoms will often grow up more slowly than others the same age. He or she may have more trouble getting used to new situations, making safe choices, or handling responsibility. Events that often mark a teen's first steps into adulthood—a summer job, a driver's license, leaving home for college—may not happen right away, or in the "normal" way. The young person may follow a different path with a different schedule, and may require many helping hands along the way.

The parents of a teen with behavioral health problems are also in transition. The clock is ticking, and they may feel helpless to provide what the child needs to survive in the world. One mother worries, "Will my son ever be able to do what a boss tells him without getting into a rage?" Another thinks, "How can my daughter go to college, when she still needs me to get her out of bed in the morning?" Meanwhile, the teen, like most teens, probably resists being told what to do. Parents in transition have the tricky, often thankless task of holding on while letting go. School is one place this will happen. At age 16 (or sooner when necessary) a child in special education becomes part of the IEP team, with the right to have a say in what kinds of training and services he or she receives. Your job as a parent in transition is to help your child learn to be a full working member of this team, planning for the shape of things to come.

Back to the Big Picture

People often ask a child, "What do you want to BE when you grow up?" A more useful question for a teen in transition might be, "How do I picture my everyday life when I'm an adult?" That picture will have several important pieces: a satisfying job (and whatever study it takes to get the job); a place to live; activities to fill free time; transportation; and a community that includes friends, loved ones, and people to give support when needed. IDEA 2004 requires the school system to develop a **transition plan** that describes the path your child intends to take after high school. It must include the training and services that will help to prepare your child for that path. However, the transition planning process can end up being little more than long, empty words on paper unless **YOU** keep everyone's eyes on the Big Picture. At every IEP meeting, you have to keep asking the team, "How does this education program get my child from here to there by the end of high school? How do these steps lead to the goals? Does the picture need to change? What are the choices? HOW ARE WE MAKING IT REAL?"

5 The Classroom-Treatment Connection
CONTINUED

More Than Work and Study

The statement about a young adult's path after high school should also contain a brief description of the plan for:

- *your child's intended form of housing;*
- *transportation;*
- *how the young adult will keep safe and healthy;*
- *who will take care of his or her daily needs; and*
- *how the young adult will be involved in the community.*

As the child gets older, this picture needs to become more detailed. The more that picture of the future comes into focus, the more your team can develop services and supports to help your child live independently.

Big-Picture Planning

One way to start creating the Big Picture of life after high school is to look back at the strengths, needs, and dreams that you and your child listed on pages 7-10. On another sheet of paper (or your computer, if you're using the CD), start filling in some more details. You and your child may choose to work on this "future story" together or separately. Think: What would an average weekday include? Ask questions such as "What kind of work setting might fit the child's strengths and personality?" (Quiet and routine? Active, with lots of variety and people nearby? Indoors or outdoors?) Does he or she want to live at home after high school? What about transportation? What about free time? Who are the people in the child's life that already give help, advice, and support? Who else and what else will need to become part of the child's life in the next few years?

NOTE: Many teens can only take this process in small doses. Thinking about the future can provoke a lot of anxiety, as well as push-pull feelings about the parent's role. ("Take care of me but get out of my life!") You may want to keep your own plan in the background at first, using it as a source of ideas as you, your child, and the rest of the team start to create the transition plan.

The Basic IDEA for Transition

Under IDEA 2004, the IEP document in effect when a child turns 16 must contain statements that cover four main elements:

- **Your child's intended path after leaving high school.** This statement will describe the child's work, education, and other life plans after high school. This might include a job, college, vocational school, or a training program.

- **Your child's transition needs as they affect the education program.** This means the IEP team must indicate what kinds of classes, training, or other experiences are necessary to meet your child's needs to prepare for this path while in high school. NOTE: This may also include services to help your child to explore different work or study choices.

- **Necessary transition services.** The IEP must list services that the school system will provide to help your child develop the skills necessary to make his or her plan a reality. In addition to academic study or training programs, these services might include special coaching for skills your child will need. Some examples might be learning how to write a resume or learning to use public transportation.

- **Non-educational agencies.** The IEP must state whether agencies in charge of certain benefits, health programs, or job training can provide services, and how to access (get help from) those services. The plan will also describe how the school will get involved in working with those agencies.

How to Stay in Touch With Your Child's Teacher(s)

At the start of the IEP period, talk to the teacher about the best ways to stay in touch. Sometimes the communication plan is built into the IEP. The method has to fit the child's age and ability to communicate on his or her own. These are a few of the choices:

Communications journal:
The parent and teacher write messages to each other in a notebook the child carries back and forth to school each day.

Regular collaborative meetings: *If a child is in crisis or is making a big transition, the parent, teacher, and other staff could meet briefly on a regular basis, such as once a month.*

Daily/Weekly Communications Sheet:
Many teachers make up a form with symbols or check-off boxes to report behavior and with room to write comments. At the bottom, the parent writes a response, signs it, and sends it back.

Keeping You Up to Date Form: *See page 40.*

Ten Things Teachers Want You to Know

1. **Most teachers aren't experts in education law.** A classroom teacher may not always understand your child's rights under IDEA 2004 or be aware of all the services your child can receive. Start by assuming they want to help, and help them figure out how to do it.

2. **Teachers work for the school system.** Like any other employees, they have to follow the school rules and carry out the decisions of their superiors.

3. **Teachers want your child to learn and be successful.** Sometimes a teacher may not understand what your child needs. Ask if the teacher would like an article or fact sheet that describes your child's disability or offers classroom ideas.

4. **Teachers want you to be involved.** They need you to help them understand your child's behavior. They need you to participate in carrying out behavior plans and solving problems. Show up for school meetings and volunteer to help, even in small ways. In the teacher's mind, you will change from a "problem parent" to a "parent partner."

5. **You will get better attention by respecting the teacher's time.** Find out how and when the teacher likes to be contacted. Schedule meetings in advance and show up on time. If possible, let the teacher know what the issues are ahead of time so he or she can be prepared.

6. **Like everybody, teachers can be nervous about change.** A teacher may resist a new method because he or she can't see how it fits into the routine. Encourage your IEP team to include any necessary teacher training in your child's plan. IDEA 2004 permits this service.

7. **Teachers want to hear from you before a small problem becomes a big problem.** "Nine times out of ten, it's a 30-second fix," says Melissa Massie, a special education supervisor. "It might just be a breakdown in communication. Write a note. If nothing happens, pick up the phone."

8. **Teachers make mistakes.** However, they don't appreciate being embarrassed in front of their bosses. Be tactful. Talk to the teacher first before going to a higher-up.

9. **Teachers like to be kept up to date.** Let them know about medication changes and events at home that might affect behavior at school.

10. **Teachers like to be praised for their efforts.** Write thank-you notes often. Send holiday cards. Tell the principal or supervisor about the teacher's good work.

Chapter 6
Insurance Companies and Social Agencies

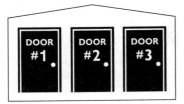

Imagine a giant building full of treatment services for your child. Which door you use to enter this building will depend on what kind of insurance benefits are available to your child.

Doorways to Health Care Benefits

When your child has trouble coping with everyday life, the goal is simple. You want to find the best help, as fast as possible, at a price your family can afford. However, in our American health care system, the path to that goal is far from simple. A lot depends on your child's behavioral health insurance benefits. **Benefits** are payments made by an insurance company for services your child receives. Many people in this country don't have benefits (also called **coverage**) for behavioral health treatment, or their insurance only pays for a limited amount of treatment. In any case, the rules for getting that treatment can be complicated. That's why you must work with behavioral health and insurance professionals to make sure your child gets the benefits he or she needs.

Imagine a giant office building that contains every sort of behavioral health treatment your child and family can receive. Imagine that inside the different offices of this building are all the organizations that provide treatment as well as all the professionals who work for these organizations. This giant building would have three front doors that might be marked with the following signs:

- **Door #1:** No insurance/No behavioral health benefits in the insurance plan
- **Door #2:** State-sponsored behavioral health insurance
- **Door #3:** Private insurance with behavioral health benefits.

Each door leads to a different series of hallways and other sets of doors that you (and your paperwork) will have to pass through in order to reach some form of treatment for your child.

No insurance plan/ No behavioral health benefits on your plan

This means you pay directly for your child's care or get help from free and low-cost services such as the health department.

If your child has no behavioral health benefits, your route may take you to free and low-cost **community resources** such as prescription drug assistance programs or clinics that charge on a **sliding scale** (according to what you can pay).

You may also need to fill out applications and visit government agencies to see if your child is eligible for free and low-cost insurance programs that help families who are uninsured, low-income, or have big medical bills. Sometimes your child will qualify to get state-sponsored insurance even if you and the other adults in the house aren't eligible.

 To learn more about how to find low-cost resources for uninsured families, or how to apply for benefits under Medicaid programs, go to Centers for Medicaid Services, www.cms.hhs.gov.

State-sponsored behavioral health insurance plan

This means that a state program pays all or part of the bills for your child's behavioral health treatment.

The state pays insurance companies called Managed Care Organizations (MCOs) and Behavioral Health Organizations (BHOs) to run different types of public health plans.

- An MCO manages plans that pay for medical services. A BHO manages plans that pay for mental (behavioral) health and substance (drug and alcohol) abuse services. If your child gets benefits from a state-sponsored plan, he or she is assigned to an MCO and a BHO.
- Your child gets routine medical care from a primary care provider (a doctor or nurse practitioner) who is part of the MCO's network.
- The BHO has its own network of providers, including a Community Mental Health Agency (CMHA) in your area.

One way that your child can get behavioral health services is through the Early and Periodic Screening, Diagnosis, and Treatment Program (EPSDT).

- Under this program, a primary care provider (PCP) must assess (check) your child for certain health needs and signs of behavioral health problems at an annual medical check-up or between check-ups if you, a teacher, or someone who works with the child notices symptoms.
- The PCP can send your child to the Community Mental Health Agency, which provides evaluation and any necessary treatment.
- You can also take your child directly to the CMHA or to a behavioral health professional in the BHO's network.

Private behavioral health insurance plan (also called "private pay")

This means your family gets benefits through a plan that you pay for yourself or that you get through an employer.

If your child is covered by private pay insurance benefits, the rules of the behavioral health plan determine where your child can get services. You may need to take your child to a primary care provider to get a referral (a doctor's order that allows your child to see a specialist). Sometimes the plan lets you take your child directly to certain behavioral health professionals (such as psychiatrists and clinical psychologists) who are in-network, without getting a referral.

- Some plans let you choose a provider who is out-of-network if your child needs a service that is not available elsewhere.

Before providing the service, your child's behavioral health professional must contact the BHO to make sure the treatment will be approved. Without this prior authorization, you could wind up having to pay the bill yourself.

- If a specific treatment is not approved by the BHO, you still have options.
- Sometimes you have to call the customer service number on your child's insurance card to correct errors in the paperwork or find out whether the BHO needs other evidence that the service is medically necessary.
- Sometimes you need to ask for a care manager, whose job it is to find solutions for difficult treatment situations.
- If that doesn't work, you may need to file an appeal (request to change the decision), according to the rules of your plan.

6 Insurance Companies and Social Agencies

CONTINUED

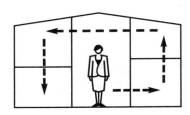

The Bottom Line on Health Care Benefits

Your child may not receive the treatment he or she needs unless you understand the basics of your child's insurance plan and get involved when things get stuck in the system.

How to Get Where You Need to Go

Inside this giant "building" full of treatment services, it's very easy to go down the wrong hallway, wander around in circles, or end up staring at a locked door. The rules of your child's insurance plan may be hard to understand and may change over time. Your child's treatment may be denied because the computer has the wrong information or because a small mistake was made in the paperwork. Often, you need to go several places to solve problems or get the right information. That's why you need to use MAPS and GUIDES along the way.

MAPS are written materials (such as a health plan membership booklet or website) that explain benefits and procedures or tell you where to go for information.

GUIDES are people who know about different parts of the process, such as customer service associates, case managers, state-sponsored advocates, or the staff in a doctor's office.

A parent often has to "pass the ball" between the treatment professionals and the insurance professionals on a child's team in order to get services. As you use maps and guides, your job is to:

- Try to get behavioral health benefits for your child if he or she doesn't have them now.

- If necessary, look for free and low-cost services that don't require health insurance.

- Learn the basic benefits of your child's plan if he or she is enrolled in one. Send in paperwork on time and do what it takes to keep your child enrolled in the plan.

- Learn the common terms used in this business so you can ask clearly for what your child needs.

- Find out who handles insurance paperwork at the provider's office. Keep a good working relationship with this person. Ask how you can help get benefits approved. Do your part.

- When the insurance plan says "no" to a treatment your child needs, don't quit until the problem is solved.

Two Words That Open Doors

Health insurance policies cover behavioral health treatments that are medically necessary, *a very important term that means the services are required to treat your child's symptoms. When your treatment team's professionals want the BHO to approve services that aren't usually covered by the plan—including more days or sessions of treatment—they have to show that the services are medically necessary. Sometimes you will have to get experts at the BHO to review your child's case. You may also have to go higher up the chain of command at the insurance company or file an appeal.*

How "Managed Care" Works

When a doctor or other clinician evaluates your child and recommends a treatment plan, you, as the parent, must agree to this plan ahead of time. If your child receives benefits, the insurance company will also get involved before treatment starts. Professionals hired by the company must agree ahead of time that the insurance plan's guidelines (rules) do in fact cover those services. This process is called a utilization review, and the professionals who do this task (often nurses and social workers) are called utilization reviewers or case managers. Sometimes another professional, such as a child psychiatrist, will review your child's case if there are questions about what your child needs. You or your child's behavioral health professional can request this added review when trying to change a decision about your child's coverage.

If the recommended treatment fits the plan's guidelines, the reviewer will authorize those services (give advance permission for the services and agree to pay for them). In the case of some benefits, such as psychotherapy, the insurance company will often authorize a certain number of sessions. Your child's therapist will have to submit another treatment plan to get more sessions approved.

Sometimes this process takes place with a phone call, but in other cases, written records have to be sent. Either way, number codes are used on the paperwork; the codes stand for certain kinds of services and reasons for needing services. Sometimes a claim can be denied because somebody accidentally used the wrong code or made a mistake entering the information into the computer. As a parent, you may need to get on the phone with staff in the behavioral health professional's office or with someone at the insurance company to fix such errors.

The insurance company that pays for services may do this review on its own, or it may use another BHO. If so, you may need to call one phone number to ask questions about benefits or solve problems and a different number for questions about billing. When problems occur, you may have to get in touch with that company using the customer service number on the ID card or in the member's handbook. Look for the mental health and substance abuse (MH/SA) number. However, the government also pays some organizations to help people who have state-sponsored health insurance when they need to work out problems with eligibility or coverage.

Behavioral health and insurance professionals have to answer three questions when making decisions about what treatment your child should receive.

6. Insurance Companies and Social Agencies
CONTINUED

Check Out the Choices

You can find out what treatment programs and services are available in your community by looking at the websites of Community Mental Health Agencies, hospitals, and other health systems in your area. One simple way to find these websites is to look in your phonebook's yellow pages under "Mental Health Services" or "Hospitals." The ads in these sections often list websites. You can also call the main number to ask about services and have information sent to you.

Your state or local NAMI affiliate may also have this information. Call NAMI's national help line, 800-950-6264, or visit www.nami.org to find your nearest affiliate.

1. What's NECESSARY?

Inside that "building" full of behavioral health services, similar problems may be treated in different ways. For example, a child going through a bad crisis may not need to be in a hospital if a program exists to treat those symptoms while the child keeps living at home. The different ways your child can get treatment are grouped into a set of categories. Below are the 12 major treatment categories, collectively called the continuum of care.

Continuum of Care

Office or outpatient clinic	Visits are usually 30-60 minutes. The number of visits per month depends on the youngster's needs.
Intensive case management	Specially trained individuals provide psychiatric, financial, legal, and medical services to help the child live successfully at home and in the community.
Home-based treatment services	A team of specially trained staff goes into a home and develops a treatment program to help the child and family.
Family support services	These are services to help families care for their child. Examples are parent training or a parent support group.
Day treatment program	An intensive outpatient program (IOP) provides psychiatric treatment with special education. The child usually attends five days per week.
Partial hospitalization (day hospital)	This provides all the treatment services of a psychiatric hospital, but the patients go home each evening.
Emergency/crisis services	These are 24-hour-per-day services for emergencies (for example, a hospital emergency room or mobile crisis team).
Respite care services	A patient stays briefly away from home with specially trained individuals.
Therapeutic group home or community residence	This therapeutic program usually includes 6 to 10 children or adolescents per home; it may be linked with a day treatment program or specialized educational program.

Crisis residence	This setting provides short-term (usually fewer than 15 days) crisis intervention and treatment. Patients receive 24-hour-per-day supervision.
Residential treatment facility	Seriously disturbed patients receive intensive and comprehensive psychiatric treatment in a campus-like setting.
Hospital treatment	Patients receive comprehensive psychiatric treatment in a hospital. Treatment programs should be specifically designed for either children or adolescents. How long your child stays depends on his or her condition and insurance benefits.

Adapted from "Facts for Families: Continuum of Care" fact sheet with permission from the American Academy of Child and Adolescent Psychiatry. For this and other fact sheets, go to www.aacap.org.

Road Map for Members

Be sure to keep the member's handbook sent by the MCO or BHO. (In some cases, you have to request a handbook by calling the customer service number on your child's ID card or asking a case manager.)

Read through the "Benefits Summary" page to get a basic idea of what the plan covers. Highlight information numbers or mark the pages with sticky notes.

Most MCOs and BHOs also have the member's handbook on their company websites. The website address will usually be listed on the ID card, or you can do an Internet search on the name of the company.

2. What's AVAILABLE?

Not all programs and services can be found in every community. These differences will affect the methods of treatment chosen by your child's team. However, if your team can show that services available in another area are medically necessary, it may be possible to use your child's benefits to pay for a service that is not available inside your health system or local area. You may need to get evidence from your child's health professional and other sources to support the view that your child needs to go somewhere else (such as a treatment center or residential program in another city).

3. What's COVERED?

Most health plans have exclusions, which are types of treatment that insurance won't pay for under certain conditions. You may have to pay a certain amount per year, called a deductible, before the health plan starts to pay. You may also have to pay a small amount, called a co-payment, for certain visits. Your plan may have an annual out-of-pocket maximum which is the highest amount of deductible and co-payment charges you are expected to pay in one year. An annual or lifetime maximum benefit is the most the insurance company will pay for a particular type of treatment over one year or during the whole time your child is covered by that plan. **NOTE: In public health plans, co-payments and annual maximums may be based on your family income. Benefits that are excluded for adults may be covered for children when the treatment is considered medically necessary.**

6 Insurance Companies and Social Agencies

CONTINUED

EZ Phone Log Tips

You can keep this log in an ordinary spiral notebook. Just be sure to include:

— *Date (month, day, and year) and time of the call.*

— *Name of the person and his or her job title.*

— *Name of company.*

— *Phone number.*

— *Issue (what you wanted).*

— *Response (what you were told or promised).*

— *Comments.*

Write neatly—you may need to show this log if you appeal a claim.

Keep A Phone Log

The best way to get results from customer service is to keep a log of "who said what and when." This creates a record of your conversations if you need to go up the chain to a higher authority or file an appeal. It also helps you keep track of issues so you can explain the problem to the next person. ("My log shows that during June, I made four calls to customer service about approving in-network benefits for this treatment. On the first call, Andrew told me….but on the next call with Amy, I was told….") Frankly, even mentioning a phone log helps to get results.

Finding a Guide With Two Names

Your path to solving problems can be very different depending on whether you have public or private health insurance.

- **If you have public insurance, state law says that you must be offered a case manager.** In addition, the state has certain agencies you can call with specific problems. The state usually pays private advocacy organizations to provide certain kinds of help.

- **If you have private-pay benefits, you don't get a case manager unless you have a specific, fairly complicated problem.** You will usually have to ask for this help, and you may even have to insist on getting it.

Let's say you have a problem getting your private insurance benefits to pay for a treatment from an out-of-network doctor. When you call the help line number on your child's ID card, you will probably have to go through an automated "menu" of selections. Finally, you reach a **customer service (or member services) representative** who will answer with a first name only. ("Hello, this is Andrew, how may I help you?")

Be Flexible

One provider suggests asking about flexible benefits *if you have private pay insurance. That means the BHO agrees that money targeted for one benefit can be used to pay for another level of care. For example, if your policy allows 30 days per year of inpatient hospital treatment, the BHO might agree to use that money to pay for 60 days of treatment in a residential program. Sometimes the BHO can just pull the money out of one pot and put it into another.*

This BHO employee is trained to look in your child's computer file, answer basic questions, and clear up routine errors. "Andrew" realizes that your problem falls outside those basic guidelines. So he puts you on hold with recorded music, and finds a supervisor. The supervisor tells him—and he tells you—that your provider needs to send in a letter with three pieces of information (we'll call them Info A, B, and C). Andrew makes notes about this solution in your child's computer file. "If you have any other problems," he says cheerfully, "just call the main number and any representative can help you. It's all in the file."

If you're lucky, that's the end of it. If you're not lucky, you have to call back again and go through the same automated system in order to reach a human voice. This time the call is taken by a different person—let's call her "Amy"—who needs to hear the whole story again. She looks in your child's computer file to see what Andrew noted last time. Amy tells you the rules clearly ask for Info D, E, and F. Just to be sure, Amy talks to her supervisor while you listen to more music. Eventually, they decide that the provider should have sent Info A and Info D. You call your provider's office to report this. It turns out the office manager sent A and D two weeks ago, but nothing happened. So you call the customer service number and it all begins again….

When the issue is complicated, you won't get far by dealing with first-name-only phone staff. BHOs have special case managers, often called care managers, who deal with unusual situations. This type of professional will usually tell you his or her first **and** last name and will often provide a direct phone number to use if you need to call back. Even better are field care managers, BHO employees who work in your community. They are familiar with both local and regional systems, so they are in the best position to tell you where to find the services your child needs. "When they say 'just call the main number,' ask if there is somebody local you can talk to," recommends one insurance company executive. "If that doesn't work, ask to talk to a supervisor who can explain how the decision was made. If you still don't understand, ask to talk to that person's supervisor." Be persistent.

"You need to find someone in the organization who can help you identify the issues and get to solutions," comments the provider. "As a parent, you need to keep asking, 'What are our rights? What are our options?' Keep pushing to get the services you feel your child needs."

Chapter 7
Coping with Crisis and Healing the Family

What is a Crisis?

A psychiatric crisis is a situation in which someone has a sudden, serious change in behavior, with overwhelming emotions, thoughts that don't make sense to others, and plans or attempts to do something that will cause serious physical harm to self or others.

Look back at page 16 for signs that mean that your child may be at risk of suicide or violence.

If your child seems to be in immediate danger of serious self-injury or violence toward someone else, your FIRST call should be to a youth Specialized Crisis Services number (see page 89).

When Things Fall Apart

Few experiences are as frightening for a parent as watching a child lose the ability to function in everyday life. Sometimes you can see the clues that a crisis is building. There might be a sharp increase in angry explosions, signs of drug and alcohol use, or self-injuries that a child tries to hide. But sometimes you suddenly face an emergency that seems to have come from nowhere. Even a strong parent who has weathered many storms can feel numb with shock, filled with rage, or helpless to meet this new challenge. A terrible thing is happening to your family. If you are worn down by a long period of living with your child's symptoms, you may feel an overwhelming wish to let the professionals take over. Indeed, others may need to care for your child briefly in an inpatient psychiatric unit (hospital) or residential treatment center (a 24-hour live-in facility). Yet now more than ever, your child and your family need you to stay involved. There are four truths any parent in an urgent situation should know:

1. **This crisis will pass.** Like any event, it has a beginning, a middle, and an end. Life may look somewhat different when it's over, but you and your family will get through the experience and go on.

2. **Your child and others in the family won't get the help they need unless YOU participate as a full member of the team.** In a crisis, professionals who don't know your child may join the team. These people have never seen your child look happy and don't know anything about the Big Picture. The action speeds up and members of the team may miss details that only you can see. You will need to ask good questions and pass the ball so that everyone gets the right information.

3. **You can't do it alone.** Feelings of guilt or shame about this event can prevent a family from reaching out to others. While it's true that sometimes people who are close to your family don't understand what you're going through, part of your job in this crisis is to figure out how to share the burden with relatives, friends, your faith community, or others who can help. To make such decisions, you may need to seek out other families who have lived through a child's crisis and who can offer advice or support.

4. **What you learn from this experience can help you head off the next crisis or handle it more quickly.** By paying attention to how the situation began, ran its course, and was resolved, you can learn the signs of a developing crisis and create a strategy to deal with it.

Violent Behavior in Children and Youth

*Most children have the occasional urge to hurt somebody or damage something. However, when a child of any age shows a **pattern** of violent behavior—even in small ways—a parent should seek help as soon as possible. A pattern means certain kinds of actions that happen over and over.*

A pattern of violence is not "just a phase" and a child won't "grow out of it" without intervention to find and treat the causes of that behavior. Talk to a health professional if you see any of these warning signs:

—*Explosive temper tantrums that put others at risk of harm,*

—*Attempts to hurt others,*

—*Threats against others (including siblings),*

—*Vandalism,*

—*Use of weapons,*

—*Cruelty toward animals,*

—*Fire-setting,*

—*Evidence of frequent thoughts about killing or injuring others.*

The Power of Planning

After Hurricane Katrina, many American families put together a crisis survival kit with basic supplies to help them get through the worst days of a natural disaster. Families who live with a child's behavioral health symptoms need a different type of crisis survival kit to use in the event a child needs emergency care. The basic supplies in this kit are four kinds of information: (1) Your child's current records, (2) emergency resources, (3) a list of questions to ask if your child needs urgent care, and (4) a family safety plan. If this information is already organized in your binder, you can react more quickly when a crisis begins.

Current records: Emergency personnel will need to know about any past clinical evaluations, medical conditions, and medications your child takes. You may also have to fill out forms with this information if your child is admitted to a hospital or other treatment facility. Make sure your child's Health History (page 22) and Medications Log (page 51) are up to date, so you can transfer information easily or show it to staff. In some cases, the staff may let you attach these summaries rather than rewriting the information.

Emergency Resources: If possible, you should call the doctor or nurse practitioner (NP) who handles your child's behavioral health needs. ***Your child may not need to go to a hospital if there are other choices available.*** In some cases, your child's doctor or NP may prescribe certain medications to treat *acute* (temporary and severe) symptoms. The state usually provides free Specialized Crisis Services for children and adolescents whose symptoms pose a serious risk of harm to themselves or others. Trained staff comes to the child's location to assess (determine by using certain rules or standards) the child's need for emergency services. This service is typically faster and less stressful than calling 911. If police answer a 911 call, officers may need to transport your child to a regular hospital emergency room; they'll then call a specialized crisis services team to determine if your child needs emergency care.

To find out about Specialized Crisis Units, ask a local mental health provider or call the nearest psychiatric or residential facility that accepts children.

7 Coping with Crisis and Healing the Family
CONTINUED

Family Safety Plan

Siblings and other family members may be at risk if your child shows symptoms of violence. Case managers can often help you form a plan for protecting family members from harm in a crisis situation.

A safety plan includes making the whole family aware of how to:

—Recognize triggers and early warning signs. *(These are events that indicate the first stages of an emergency.)*

—Lower the tension. *(This can mean giving each family member an "assignment." For example, an adult may be assigned to hold the child with a firm, soothing grasp, while a young sibling may be assigned to leave the area immediately.)*

—Recognize the worst-case scenario and do the assigned task. *(Example: "Mary goes across the street to Mrs. Smith and asks her to call the crisis unit.")*

—Recognize the resolution. *(Know when the crisis has passed and figure out how to help prevent another episode.)*

Twenty Questions to Ask If Your Child Needs In-Patient Or Residential Treatment

1. How will treatment at this facility help my child's symptoms?
2. What are other options for treating these symptoms? How do the options compare?
3. Will my child be placed in an inpatient unit that is specifically designed to treat children and teens?
4. Will my child be admitted and treated by a child and adolescent psychiatrist?
5. How long is the average stay on this unit? How is this decision made, and by whom?
6. What professional will evaluate my child? What types of tests will be used? Who will explain the evaluation results to me, and when?
7. What activities will be part of my child's day? How will my child keep up with schoolwork?
8. Is family counseling part of this program? What will we need to do?
9. What should I pack for my child? Can my child have comfort items such as a favorite stuffed toy or picture from home?
10. What are the visiting policies? When and how often may I get information about my child between visits? May I talk to my child by phone?
11. What behavior management systems are used to enforce rules? What happens if my child doesn't comply? What consequences are used?
12. Does the staff use restraint methods? Please explain how and when.
13. Are staff allowed to use medications on an as-needed basis to calm children who are agitated or aggressive?
14. How often will the psychiatrist see my child for medication management?
15. What are the roles of others on the treatment team?
16. How much will treatment cost per day? Does this hospital accept our insurance benefits?
17. What will happen if the insurance company denies coverage and inpatient treatment is still necessary?
18. How will I be involved in my child's hospital treatment, including decisions about medications, discharge, and after-care treatment?
19. Once our child is discharged, what plans will be made for his or her ongoing treatment?
20. Will a case manager be able to help us create a family safety plan?

The Bigger Picture: Family Recovery

Most health care systems and health insurance plans are designed around a simple goal. They provide (or pay for) direct treatment to people with illnesses in order to help them get well. Unfortunately, that goal does not always fit the needs of children with behavioral health problems and their families. Professionals on a treatment team usually receive payment for providing services to the affected child, meaning the child who shows symptoms of a disorder. But the truth is that everybody in the family can be deeply affected by the stress and turmoil a child's symptoms create. Siblings may feel overlooked by their exhausted parents or embarrassed in front of peers by a family that isn't "normal." Parents and relatives may blame each other for the symptoms or argue bitterly about how to handle the child. Harsh words spoken in a crisis can be hard to take back when things settle down. The tension of coping day after day can break up marriages and damage relationships.

Yet many families who struggle with serious behavioral health problems will become stronger, closer, and better able to care for one another. No two stories of family recovery are alike, but a common theme is that each family member was able to get the support he or she needed to find a "new normal." So, part of your job as a parent advocate is to keep one eye on the Bigger Picture of how your family can stay as healthy and stable as possible. You may have to keep pushing your team to "think family" when building your child's treatment plan. You may have to look for other services. Even more important, you will need to make contact with other families, programs, or people in your community that can lift you up when you're down and keep you going when you feel like quitting. Steps to consider:

Pay attention to signs that others in the family (including yourself) may need professional help. Certain behavioral health problems can often show up in several members of the same family. For example, genetic research has shown that about 25 percent of people with depression have a parent or close relative with depression. A person with one parent who has bipolar disorder has a 30 percent chance of showing those symptoms; the chances rise to 70 percent if both parents have the disorder.

The constant demands of dealing with a difficult child can also take their toll. Yet many parents fail to seek treatment for their own symptoms until they reach the crisis stage. Some feel their own needs shouldn't matter. Others may fear losing custody of a child if they admit to feeling out of control. They may worry that health or school professionals will not treat them seriously if they share information about their own diagnosis. Sometimes they don't have insurance

---

Support for Families

Consider looking for respite services that can give you a short break to spend time with your spouse, your other children, or yourself. Ask about respite programs at mental health centers in your community. Funding programs may be available. For help finding respite programs, try the ARCH National Respite Network, www.chtop.org/ARCH.html or call the Family Respite Network at 888-269-7855. You can also get money to pay for respite care through a Family Support Program in your community. Call toll-free 800-535-9725 to find the nearest program coordinator.

For support and training from other families who deal with behavioral health problems, go to www.nami.org or call the HelpLine at 800-950-6264.

7 Coping with Crisis and Healing the Family
CONTINUED

Stop, Look, and Listen

Mpower: Musicians for Mental Health *is a website that uses the influence of top recording artists to give teens and older children solid information, real-life stories and practical advice on behavioral health problems. Topics range from disorders such as depression and anorexia to self-esteem issues, stress, and coping with divorce.*

The website is sponsored by the National Mental Health Association, which offers a wealth of information on disorders, treatments, and mental health issues. Go to www.nmha.org or call toll-free 800-969-NMHA.
Información disponible en español.

A "listening booth" on the site links to home pages of established as well as emerging bands. Go to www.mpoweryouth.org/411.htm for more information.

---

benefits to cover their own behavioral health care. Even so, parents who ignore their own symptoms are setting themselves up for a disaster that can make all the other fears come true. Your child needs for you to be whole, healthy, and able to function. If coping with everyday life becomes difficult, talk to your doctor or look for behavioral health treatment. Try to schedule a session with your child's therapist to talk about ways to handle the stress of dealing with your child. **If you are in a serious crisis and need to talk to a counselor, call the Suicide Hotline, toll-free 800-273-TALK.**

Siblings of a child with behavioral health problems are also at risk if they carry the same genetic predisposition (inherited tendency to develop an illness). In any case, they can feel deep conflicts between loving a brother or sister with a serious disorder and being angry about the unfair demands of the situation. Some children act out to get a parent's attention, while others try to be the "extra-good child" who doesn't cause trouble. Neither response will be healthy in the long run.

Try to include family counseling in your child's treatment plan. Part of that counseling needs to focus on practical strategies for making sure that siblings get a fair share of attention from parents, have a way to talk over their questions or fears, and stay safe during a crisis. Lee Fitzgibbons, PhD, and Cherry Pedrick, RN, co-authors of **Helping Your Child with OCD** (New Harbinger Publications, Oakland, CA, 2003) recommend that parents try to schedule at least 15 minutes per day of YAMA–"you and me alone" time–with each child in the family. It can be as simple as a walk down the street or a chat while cooking dinner. The important thing is to make it a regular ritual the child can count on. Meanwhile, be alert for signs that you should seek professional help for the sibling: A sudden change in sleep habits or appetite, poor concentration, low self-esteem, frequent crying or worrying, difficulty separating from parents, frequent physical problems such as headaches or stomachaches, or loss of interest in activities.

Widen your family's circle of support. Families that bounce back from severe problems usually have a support network that plugs them into a caring community and provides help when needed. Many people want to lend a hand–or cooperate with you to find ways you can help each other. Sometimes the trick is figuring out what kinds of help will strengthen your family, and matching those needs with the support each person is able to give. For example, a school cafeteria worker may be willing to nudge your child into making better food choices. You might partner with another family to take turns providing respite care. An elderly neighbor might watch out her window to make sure your child gets safely off the bus. The wider your circle, the smaller the burden each person has to carry, and the more your child will become an independent part of his or her community.

Your Family's Circle of Support

This worksheet can help you think about people, groups, and programs that might offer practical or emotional support to your family. A strong circle of support that relies on many sources has the power to keep on growing. Ask professionals on your team for ideas. If possible, get your child or children to help you list the people who influence them to do the right thing and provide help they appreciate.

People and organizations:	Phone numbers and e-mail addresses:	What kinds of help this person or group can provide:
Relatives:		
Friends:		
Neighborhood and business community:		
School staff:		
Faith community:		
Sources for paid, volunteer, or cooperative respite care:		
Community programs:		
Social agencies:		
Family advocacy organizations:		
Support groups:		

Chapter 8: Glossary

Accommodations and modifications (Education). Changes made in a regular education program to help a child make educational progress. Children must meet certain criteria to be eligible for these changes (See **504 Plan**).

Affected child. A child who shows symptoms of a behavioral health or other disorder.

Annual (IEP) goal. An educational goal that the school system expects your child to reach by the end of a year, as part of his or her Individualized Education Program (IEP).

Annual IEP review. A meeting to review a child's Individualized Education Program and make any necessary changes in goals, placement, or services within the next year.

Annual or lifetime maximum benefit. The maximum amount that your health-care plan will pay for treatment of a particular kind of health problem, either per year (annually) or during the entire time your plan is in effect.

Annual out-of-pocket maximum. The maximum amount that you will be required to pay per year for certain types of treatment under the terms of your health insurance plan.

Appeal. A formal request for a decision to be changed by a higher authority.

Areas of need (Education). Broad categories in which your child needs to improve in order to make progress in school, as determined by the IEP team and included in the IEP document.

Assess. To evaluate a person's medical, behavioral, or educational condition in order to determine what services the person needs.

Assessment team (Education). A team of school staff or consultants assigned by the school to evaluate a child. For behavioral health issues, the team usually includes a psychologist and may include specialists in certain disorders.

Authorization, pre-authorization, prior-authorization (Insurance). Approval given by the insurance company for a treatment that is shown to be medically necessary and covered by the person's health care benefits.

Behavioral Health Organization. An insurance company that manages benefit plans for mental (behavioral) health or substance (drug and alcohol) abuse treatment.

Benefits. Also called "coverage." The contract between an insurance provider and the insured person that obligates the insurance company to pay for certain medical or behavioral health treatments.

Black-box warning. A Food and Drug Administration (FDA) warning that alerts doctors to a possibly serious side effect or complication that might be caused by giving a medication under certain conditions.

Care manager (Insurance). A type of case manager for a health insurance plan whose job it is to help people find options for getting treatment approved or to solve unusual problems with the benefits plan.

Case manager. 1) A health or social agency professional who helps set up services for a child and his or her family. May also provide counseling; 2) An employee of the insurance company, often a nurse or social worker, who pre-authorizes treatment; 3) a school staff member who coordinates the services received by a child in special education.

Certified or **certification.** Eligible (allowed) to receive special education services. A child has to be certified under one of IDEA 2004 law's 13 disabilities categories in order to receive special education services.

Child Find. A program provided by every school system to assess children aged 3 through 5 who are likely to develop problems or delays in learning.

Claim (Insurance). A request to get a certain service or treatment paid by the insurance company.

Clinical diagnosis. A health professional's description of a problem, made after an evaluation is performed.

Clinician. A professional who evaluates your child (usually a clinical psychologist or licensed clinical social worker); may also provide therapy.

CMHA (Community Mental Health Agency). A large mental health center that has a contract to provide services to people who are enrolled in public health insurance plans; sometimes called a Community Mental Health Organization (CMHO). A CMHA is located in each county.

Glossary

Community resources. Agencies, organizations, and programs that provide services for people with different types of needs.

Comorbid diagnosis. An additional or "secondary" diagnosis when a person meets the criteria for more than one disorder.

Comprehensive assessment. See "**School evaluation.**"

Confidential information. Information about a patient that a health professional cannot tell police, employers, or others not involved in the person's treatment except under certain conditions.

Consent. Legal permission.

Continuum of care. The span of care options available for behavioral health patients, ranging from a short office visit to inpatient hospital treatment.

Co-payment. A small amount you must pay when you visit a health-care provider. Varies according to the health plan.

Coverage. Also called "benefits." The contract between an insurance company and the insured person, promising to pay for certain treatments under certain conditions.

Criteria (one criterion, many criteria). Standards that must be met in order to be included in a certain category, usually for the purpose of qualifying to receive certain services.

Cumulative Record (CR). A child's permanent school record.

Customer Services (or member services) representative. An insurance company employee that answers routine questions or solves problems by phone.

Deductible. The amount of money you must pay out-of-pocket before your insurance plan will begin to pay for certain types of services.

Diagnosis. The overall term that health professionals use to describe a problem. A behavioral health diagnosis is reached after an evaluation that may include conversations with you, your child, and others, as well as tests, examinations, or laboratory studies.

Disability or disabling condition. A condition that interferes with a child's ability to learn or function at the same level as other children of the same age.

Drug interactions. Possible problems that may occur when one drug is used at the same time as another drug.

DSM (*Diagnostic and Statistical Manual of Mental Disorders*). A publication of the American Psychiatric Association that lists and describes behavioral health disorders. Health care professionals use the DSM categories to diagnose illnesses.

Due process rights. Procedures that must be followed in order to appeal a decision made by an organization, such as the school system or a mental health center.

Early and Periodic Screening, Diagnosis, and Treatment program (EPSDT). A public health insurance program aimed at finding, diagnosing, and treating problems in children.

Early intervention services. Services available to help children from birth to age 3 who have medical, behavioral, or developmental problems.

Educational impact. The effect of a disability on how a child makes progress in school compared to others of the same age.

Eligibility criteria. Standards a person must meet in order to qualify to receive services.

Eligibility meeting. A meeting of the school Individualized Education Program, or IEP team, to determine whether a child is eligible to receive special education services. An IEP team always includes the parent if he or she is willing and able to be involved.

Evaluation. The process of looking at a person's condition or behavior in order to find out what the problem is. An evaluation can include conversations with you, your child, and others; a physical examination; other tests; and laboratory studies.

Evidence. A set of facts that can be observed and measured.

Exclusions (Insurance). Types of treatment that an insurance plan will not pay for under certain conditions.

Expected progress (Education). How much educational or developmental progress the state expects a child of a certain age to make under typical circumstances.

Extended School Year Program (ESY). An Individualized Education Program developed for the summer months in order to help a child keep up with the progress he or she has made during the school year.

Chapter 8 — Glossary, CONTINUED

Facilitator. A person who runs or directs a meeting.

Family advocacy organization. An organization that provides information, training, or support to families, and works to influence the public, legislators, or government agencies on their behalf.

Family Education Rights and Privacy Act (FERPA). A Federal law regulating how a child's school records can be used.

FAPE (Free Appropriate Public Education). Your child's right, under the federal IDEA 2004 law, to an education "designed to meet his or her unique needs." Guarantees the right to special educational services when the regular education program cannot meet a child's needs because of a disability.

Field care manager (Insurance). A special case manager employed by a Managed Care Organization or Behavioral Health Organization who is based in the local community.

504 Plan. An educational plan that lists accommodations and modifications that will help a child who meets certain criteria to make progress in a regular education program. Some children with behavioral health disorders who do not qualify for special education services under the IDEA 2004 law will qualify for 504 Plan accommodations.

Flexible benefits. An agreement by the insurance company that money targeted to pay for one type of health plan benefit (for example, in-patient hospital treatment) can be used to pay for another level of care (such as residential treatment).

Genetic predisposition. A tendency to develop an illness that is inherited through one or both parents. A predisposition means a person *may* develop that illness, and so should be watched carefully for symptoms.

Genetic traits. Physical and mental qualities or conditions a person inherits.

Good-faith effort (Education). An effort on the part of the parent(s) or school to be fair, sincere, and involved.

Guidelines (Insurance). Rules set up to determine the conditions under which certain treatment services will be approved for payment by an insurance plan.

Health history. A form that contains basic information about a person's medical history. This will usually include physical diseases, behavioral health issues, medications, allergies, immunizations, family health history, and developmental history.

IDEA 2004 (Individuals with Disabilities Education Improvement Act of 2004). A federal law that guarantees the right to educational services for students with disabilities aged 3 through 21 (or through the end of the school year in which an eligible student turns 22).

IEP (Individualized Education Program). A program of educational services for a student with a disability. In the school system, this term is often used to refer to 1) a meeting to certify a child for special education services; 2) the education plan written at this meeting; and 3) the legal document that describes the program.

IEP document. A legal agreement, signed by the school system representative and parent(s), that describes goals, placement, and services to be provided for a child with a disability.

Impact on educational performance. See "Educational impact."

Individualized Family Service Plan. A plan developed by a social agency to provide services to a child or family.

In-network provider. A member of a group of health care providers whom a patient is allowed to use under the terms of a health insurance plan.

Intake interview or appointment. The first appointment with a new health professional or social agency. At an intake interview, you give information or discuss symptoms.

Inpatient psychiatric unit. A special unit in a hospital where patients with severe behavioral health problems stay 24 hours per day while receiving treatment.

Local Education Agency (LEA) representative. The school official at an IEP meeting who has the power to make the final agreement between you and the school system about your child's educational program.

Managed Care Organization (MCO). An insurance company that the state pays to run a public medical health insurance plan.

Glossary

Medically necessary. Treatments that are necessary in order for a patient to be appropriately treated for his or her symptoms.

Member's handbook. A handbook that sums up the benefits that an insurance plan provides, as well as contact information such as providers' phone numbers and information numbers. Also available on the company's website in most cases.

Mental health/Substance abuse (MH/SA) telephone number. A phone number (listed in the handbook and on a health insurance ID card) that a person must call to get help with questions or problems relating to behavioral health insurance benefits.

Mood Disorders. Disorders that affect a person's ability to regulate emotions. Examples: Depression, Bipolar Disorder.

Nurse Practitioner (NP). A registered nurse (RN) who has done further advanced training in patient care. An NP can provide many of the same services as a doctor, including ordering tests and prescribing medicine. An NP with special training in psychiatric disorders may be called a Licensed Psychiatric Nurse Practitioner.

Objectives (also known as **data points**). In an IEP, specific steps that describe what a child must learn or accomplish in order to master a stated goal.

Obligate. Require. If the school system representative signs an agreement with you, the school is legally obligated to do what it says it will do.

Off-label. A drug prescribed for a condition or a type of patient it was not originally intended to treat. This means that the United States Food and Drug Administration (FDA) has not yet approved a drug for a certain use in a certain patient group, but a doctor may prescribe it anyway based on his or her own experience as well as the experience of other doctors and researchers.

Out-of-network. A care provider whose services are not on the list of a certain insurance company's contracted providers.

Over-the-counter medication. A medication that can be sold without a prescription from a doctor.

Parent advocate. A parent who is involved, aware, and active in the management of his or her child's care and who speaks up for the child's best interests.

Pediatrician. A doctor who specializes in children's overall health care.

PDR (Physician's Desk Reference). A reference book that lists information about all FDA-approved medications.

Premium. The amount you are expected to pay every month to your health-care plan, whether or not your child sees a provider.

Present level of performance. A portion of the IEP document that describes your child's current ability to function and make educational progress in school.

Primary care doctor. Sometimes known as a family doctor, family practice doctor, or primary care provider; a doctor that sees patients for general health care needs. A pediatrician or family physician may serve as a child's primary care doctor.

Prior Authorization. See **Authorization**.

Private pay insurance plan. A health insurance plan that you pay for yourself or that you get through an employer.

Professional. A person who is paid to provide services.

Provider. An individual or organization that provides medical or behavioral health services.

Psychiatric crisis. A situation in which a person has a sudden, severe change in behavior that creates a serious risk of harm to that person or someone else.

Psychiatric medications. Drugs prescribed by a doctor or nurse practitioner (NP) to treat behavioral health problems.

Psychiatrist. A medical doctor (MD) who has done several years of extra training in diseases and disorders of the mind. A psychiatrist can prescribe medicines.

Psychologist. A doctor (not an MD, but a PhD or PsyD) who has many years of training in dealing with mental, emotional, or behavioral problems. May do evaluations or therapy, but cannot prescribe medicines.

Referral. A primary care provider's order that will allow your child to see a specialist under the terms of your health insurance plan.

Release form. A form that you sign giving permission for one health or educational professional to share information with another professional or organization.

Chapter 8 — Glossary, CONTINUED

Residential treatment center. A facility where a person receives behavioral health or substance abuse treatment 24 hours a day.

Respite services. A worker or organization that provides temporary care for a person with an illness so regular caregivers, such as parents or other family members, can have a break.

Response to Intervention (RTI). Evidence of methods a school has tried in order to deal with a child's problem in the regular classroom.

Rule-out (Education). A condition that would disqualify a child from being certified as having a disability under IDEA 2004. For example, if the main reason for a child's lack of progress is poor attendance at school, a behavioral health issue alone would not be enough to qualify that child to receive special educational services.

School evaluation. Also called a "comprehensive assessment." An evaluation performed by the school system; this evaluation examines many areas of a child's behavior, abilities, and school performance.

Service coordinator. If a child is eligible for early intervention services because of a medical, behavioral, or developmental problem, a person called a service coordinator is assigned to help the family create a plan for getting treatment and other services.

Sliding scale. A system in which people are charged fees according to what they can afford to pay.

Special education. Services and methods used to educate students with disabilities who qualify under the federal IDEA 2004 law.

Specialized Crisis Services. A unit of trained staff that comes to a child's location to assess his or her need for emergency care.

Standardized assessment tools. Tests commonly used to evaluate behavioral health or educational problems. Some typical standard assessment tools include cognitive and adaptive tests, psychological evaluations, developmental evaluations, and educational evaluations.

State-only insurance. A state-run program to allow people without other behavioral health insurance to get treatment at a local Community Mental Health Agency.

Supplemental Security Income (SSI). Payments the federal government makes to children and adults who meet certain criteria for having a disability.

Symptoms. Signs of disease that may include physical changes, thoughts, feelings, and behaviors.

System representative. See **LEA representative**.

System of care. A community network that brings together public and private organizations such as schools, health providers, churches and social agencies to create an individualized package of services and supports that will be most effective in meeting a family's needs.

Test battery. A series of tests to help determine your child's needs.

Timeline. The time frame within which a person or organization must respond to the action taken by another person or organization.

Titration. The process of increasing a person's medication dosage from a small amount of a drug to a larger dose over a period or days or weeks.

Therapeutic dose. The amount of a drug or medicine that is effective for the patient.

Therapist. A person licensed by the state to give treatment for physical, behavioral health, and developmental disorders.

Transition. A term used in education law to mean a period of years between the late teens and early twenties, when a young person's task is to gain the skills needed for independent living.

Trauma. (Behavioral health). A serious, negative event in a person's life that can affect behavior, emotions and physical health. Examples: Sexual abuse, family violence, death of a close relative, or involvement in a natural disaster.

Utilization review, Utilization reviewer. The process by which insurance companies decide whether certain health services are covered by a person's health insurance plan. The reviewers, often nurses or social workers, are employed by the company.

Chapter 9: Where to Learn More

Other National Resources

Anxiety Disorders Association of America
www.adaa.org
Describes anxiety disorders, treatments, and common co-occurring issues. Links to www.gotanxiety.org, an excellent ADAA-sponsored website for college students.

Autism Society Of America
www.autism-society.org
Facts about autism and latest treatment options; ASA chapters listed by state.

Child & Adolescent Bipolar Foundation
www.bpkids.org
www.depressedteens.com
Includes mood charts, on-line support groups, and databases of local support groups.

Children and Adults with Attention Deficit/Hyperactivity Disorder (CHADD)
www.chadd.org
Database of local chapters and support groups; facts about ADHD in children and adults.

Foundation for Children with Behavioral Challenges
www.explosivekids.org
Information and support groups for parents dealing with easily frustrated, inflexible, or explosive children.

Jason Foundation
www.jasonfoundation.com
Provides education and training for students and families on prevention of suicide. Also includes toll-free help line 800-SUICIDE for youth in crisis.

Juvenile Bipolar Research Foundation
www.jbrf.org
Among the offerings on this site are brief screening tools that help families know when to seek help.

More Advanced Persons with Autism and Asperger's Syndrome (MAAP)
www.maapservices.org
Information, resources, and links to latest research.

NAMI (National Alliance on Mental Illness)
www.nami.org
800-950-6264
See next page.

National Alliance for Research on Schizophrenia and Depression (NARSAD)
www.narsad.org
Facts about all major mental illnesses; information on genetic links to childhood disorders.

Obsessive-Compulsive Foundation
www.ocfoundation.org
Facts about OCD. Links to a webzine and website called "*Organized Chaos*," produced by and for teens and young adults with OCD.

Tourette Syndrome Association
www.tsa-usa.org
Includes "**That Darn Tic**," newsletter for children and young adult newsletter "*It's Not Just for Kids Anymore*."

Check out the *Team Up* website for information and resources.

You can also order ***Team Up for Your Child*** e-book version, plus worksheets on CD, books, teaching aids, and more. Go to www.meltonhillmedia.com.

The Nation's Voice on Mental Illness

About NAMI (National Alliance on Mental Illness)

NAMI is the nation's largest grassroots mental health organization, with affiliates in every state and more than 1100 communities. NAMI is dedicated to improving the lives of persons with mental illness, their families, and their communities through programs that offer education, support, and public advocacy. For more information contact NAMI, www.nami.org, or call the toll-free help line, 800-950-6264.

NAMI Tennessee provides education, support, and public advocacy programs throughout the state through its Nashville-based headquarters and its 40-plus affiliates from Memphis to Mountain City.

A free, six-session course for "primary care providers" of children and teens with behavioral health problems is provided by NAMI Tennessee and most other affiliates in the nation. Parents, grandparents, aunts, uncles, respite care providers, or foster parents find a safe, supportive place to share experiences with other adults who also care for children with biologically-based illnesses such as ADHD, Anxiety and Panic Disorders, Bipolar Disorder, Conduct Disorder, Depression, Eating Disorders, Obsessive-Compulsive Disorder, Post-Traumatic Stress Disorder, and Schizophrenia. Specially-trained volunteers who are also primary care providers for children with mental illness teach all classes. The course covers:

- Symptoms and treatment for specific disorders.
- Problem management and handling conflict.
- Working as allies with the school system.
- Organization and record keeping.
- Understanding the juvenile justice system.
- Coping and self-care techniques.

Contact: **NAMI Tennessee**
1101 Kermit Drive
Nashville, TN 37217
615-361-6608 or 800-467-3589
www.namitn.org

Team Up for Your Child workshops for families can be arranged through your school or health provider. Contact meltonhillmedia@yahoo.com.

Many local **NAMI** affiliates also provide regular support groups for family members of adults with mental illness and primary caregivers of children with mental illness. For information on these and other **NAMI** programs or to find the nearest affiliate, contact:

NAMI
2107 Wilson Blvd., Suite 300
Arlington, VA 22201-3042
Toll-free help line, 800-950-6264 (950-NAMI)
www.nami.org

Team Up for Your Child is a publication of

Melton Hill Media
9119 Solway Ferry Road
Oak Ridge, TN 37830
www.meltonhillmedia.com
meltonhillmedia@yahoo.com